Recruiting Strategies for Christian Schools

To Mark & Linda:
Thank you for your friendship, encouragement and for counsel in time of need.
We love you.
Dennis & Carol.

How to Recruit and Retain Students

Dennis M. Demuth, Ph.D.
Carol M. Demuth, Ed.D.

PUBLISHED BY:
DEL Publications
5747 South Utica, Suite 101
Tulsa, OK 74105-8038

All scriptures contained herein, unless otherwise noted, are from the King James Version of the Bible.

Library of Congress Cataloging Card Number 91-090682
Demuth, Dennis M.
Recruiting Strategies for Christian Schools / Dennis M. Demuth, Carol M. Demuth
p. cm.
Includes Index
ISBN 1-88075-00-1

Printed and bound in the United States of America

For more information about other Christian School Publications write or call:

Demuth Enterprises, Ltd.
5747 South Utica, Suite 101
Tulsa, OK 74105-8038
(918) 749-2157

Table of Contents

About the Authors

Dennis M. Demuth, Ph.D., has been involved in Christian Education since 1972. Dr. Demuth served as Superintendent of Schools for Victory Christian School for the past nine years and is currently Director of Christian Education at Victory Christian Center, Tulsa, Oklahoma. He has served as adjunct professor in Christian School Administration at Oral Roberts University for the past ten years. He was instrumental in the founding of the International Christian Accrediting Association (ICAA) and assisted in the development and implementation of standards for the pilot ICAA accreditation program. His book, *Legal Requirements for Christian Schools*, is being used by Christian schools all 50 states. Two other works in preparation, *Spirit-Directed Model of Education* and *Kingdom Principles for Christian Educators*, are being written out of a deep concern for incorporating the uncompromised Word of God in Christian education. Dr. Demuth's desire is for all Christian schools to develop to full maturity so every student can achieve his highest potential.

Carol M. Demuth, Ed.D., received her degree in higher education from Oklahoma State University. She has been active in Christian education for many years, serving as teacher and administrator. She has co-authored several books with her husband, Dennis. Her most recent works include, *GranDees: A School-Based Volunteer Program* and *Legal Requirements for Christian Schools.* A work in preparation, *Spirit-Directed Discipline* is designed for Christians educators who desire to train students to be self-disciplined.

Acknowledgements

We wish to express our appreciattion to the dedicated secretaries, teachers, and administrators of Victory Christian School who have served as co-laborers.

> **"Now he that planteth and he that watereth are one: and every man shall receive his own reward according to his own labour.**
>
> **"For we are labourers together with God: ye are God's husbandry, ye are God's building"** (1 Cor. 3:8,9).

We must also extend our appreciation to Pastor Billy Joe Daugherty for faithfully running with the vision of Victory Christian School.

> **"And the LORD answered me, and said, Write the vision, and make it plain upon tables, that he may run that readeth it.**
>
> **"For the vision is yet for an appointed time, but at the end it shall speak, and not lie: though it tarry, wait for it; because it will surely come, it will not tarry"** (Hab. 2:2,3).

Special recognition is given to Mark Turner, Church Administrator; Mike McCutchin, Director of Finances; David Hand, Don Petry and Dave Wagner of the Oral Roberts University Educational Fellowship, and Marilyn Price for her encouragement and editing.

"For by wise counsel thou shalt make thy war: and in multitude of counsellors there is safety" (Prov. 24:6).

Preface

God has said by His Spirit, "In these last days I am raising up an Army that will go out and possess the land. Part of this mighty Army are the children who are being trained within Christian schools. These young people will be for signs and wonders that will cause many to come to acknowledge Christ as Lord. They are the ones who will do mighty exploits for God.

"The students in these schools will go out under the anointing of the Holy Spirit, empowered to do the works of Jesus, knowing their authority in Christ and using the Word with great effectiveness. These students will not boast or glory in their own skill or wisdom; rather, they will glory in the fact that they know and understand Me, and that I am a rewarder of those who diligently seek Me.

"From these schools will come a new generation of students who will move in and take over the schools, churches, universities and corporations and will literally do the ministry of Jesus.

"My Spirit is searching this world over, looking for men and women whose hearts are humbled before Me, who are willing to be obedient to the voice of My Spirit. It will be these men and women whom I will call to give birth to a new generation of Christian schools."

This book presents proven strategies found to be effective in recruiting and retaining students for this end-time Army.

This book is about building quality Christian schools. As you read this book, we expect it to become a key resource tool in recruiting and retaining students. Ultimately, we sense it will help you fulfill the will of God in your Christian school.

Drs. Dennis and Carol Demuth

A Continual Concern 1

Many people have the idea that just because they open a Christian school in their community, the people in the community will beat a path to their door and enroll their children. The fact is, this is not so! (A.A. Baker, 1979, p. 115).

Student recruitment is a continual concern, regardless of whether your school is in its first year or fifteenth year of operation. Unlike public schools, where students come from assigned attendance areas and are compelled to attend based on law, Christian schools must go out and recruit students. For some schools, survival depends upon aggressive recruiting. For others, it is a matter of retaining students already enrolled. According to officials from Christian school associations, Christian schools are working harder at recruiting and retaining students than ever before.

Quality Leads to Quantity

Ask any school administrator, "What is the number one hindrance to full enrollment?" Nine out of every ten answers will point to "the high cost of tuition."

Some administrators reason, "If we could reduce our tuition, we could enroll more students." Lowering tuition may result in more student enrollments, but most schools cannot reduce tuition significantly enough to draw the needed students to offset the income loss. In fact, most schools must raise their tuition yearly just to keep up with inflation.

What then is the solution? Keeping the cost of operating a Christian school as low as possible is a must. But, lower cost without quality programs will not sustain the school. Adding to the quality of the school has the greatest influence on recruiting and retaining students. Regardless of the size of the school or the number of years it has existed, the best strategy for recruiting and retaining students is offering a quality Christian school.

Schools just getting started have an advantage over established schools; new schools can learn from experiences of others and avoid costly mistakes. They can plan for success from the very first day. The larger the school and the longer it has been in existence, the greater will be the amount of effort and time it takes to improve. Large and established schools are much like a huge oil tanker; it takes much energy and time to turn the ship - seemingly forever. However, it will turn if the helmsman sets a steady course.

Regardless of the age or size of the school, the suggestions contained in this book provide a course of action for launching an effective student recruitment and retention program.

Implementing a few good strategies will help turn around a declining enrollment and place a school on the course to success. For a school already experiencing growth and prosperity, one or two good ideas will increase its stability through difficult waters.

Growth is a Biblical Expectation

Anyone can start a Christian school. All one needs is someone to teach, a curriculum to teach and, of course, someone to do the teaching. When we first became involved in Christian education in the early 70's, there was an average of three new Christian schools opening per week. This rate climbed to three per day in the early 80's. Although the rate of new schools starting remains high, many Christian schools have fallen by the wayside; others are struggling to keep their doors open - finding that it is much easier to get a school going than to keep it growing.

All Christian schools planted under the inspiration of God are expected to grow. Jesus believed in growth. He likened the Kingdom of God unto a mustard plant, which begins as a small seed and grows into a large tree (Matt. 13:31,32).

Growth means progress and development. It means being receptive to change. Just because something worked once doesn't mean it will work the next time. For example, a policy may be effective one year, but given a different group of students and parents, the policy may need to be changed. Adjusting when necessary is a positive characteristic of successful schools: a mark of maturity.

Mature Christian schools are those bearing much fruit (John 15:8)

> **"Herein is my Father glorified, that ye bear much fruit; so shall ye be my disciples,"**

and having their fruit last (John 15:16) ,

> **"Ye have not chosen me, but I have chosen you, and ordained you, that ye should go and bring forth fruit, and that your fruit should remain: that whatsoever ye shall ask of the Father in my name, he may give it you."**

A Christian school will bear fruit to the degree it grows. Growth requires resources. There are numerous resources available to every Christian school. This book will help to identify these resources and show how to utilize them in formulating recruiting and retention strategies.

Enrollment Philosophy

How large of a school do you envision - 50, 100, 300, 1000 students? We have helped schools start with fewer than 15 students. Very few schools start as large schools; they usually begin with less than 100 students.

Zechariah said, **"For who hath despised the day of small beginnings?"** (Zec. 4:10). Jesus started with two small fish and five loaves and fed more than 5,000. A small beginning with His blessing will be multiplied.

Victory Christian School in Tulsa, Oklahoma, opened with 226 students and in six years grew to 835 students. The school is looking towards the day when it will minister to 3,000 students. Can a school with a vision for 100 students be as successful as a school with 1,000 students? The answer is yes. Producing a successful school goes beyond numbers alone. Fulfilling God's plan for the school is the real measure of success, whether the school size is 10, 100, or 1,000.

The gateway to success begins by determining your target population. The enrollment philosophy of a school dictates its target population.

Most Christian schools stick to one of three enrollment philosophies - evangelistic open enrollment, Christian kids only, or Christian kids who meet special requirements. The more restrictive the target population, the greater must be the school's recruiting efforts.

Evangelistic Open Enrollment

This is the least restrictive enrollment philosophy. Any student can enroll as long as he agrees to meet school enrollment standards. The major advantage of this policy is it provides the greatest number of potential prospects. It also provides the opportunity to reach parents and students with the Gospel and win them to Christ.

Christian Kids Only

This approach is more restrictive than an evangelistic open enrollment philosophy, for it seeks to recruit those students who are from Christian families. These schools function within a traditional doctrinal position acceptable to most churches in the community.

Often, the rationale for this approach is, "If we recruit students from non-Christian homes, they will have an adverse influence upon Christian students already enrolled, and as a result, the school will not be able to maintain its Christian standards." Those who select this approach should know that Christian schools have many of the same problems as secular schools, even when all the students profess to be Christians. As long as students, staff and parents are human, there will be imperfection.

Special Requirements

Many schools go one step further; they add special requirements beyond being a Christian or coming from a Christian home. Some schools accept only children from the sponsoring church, churches, or denomination; others may require agreement with a specific doctrinal position. Some may require prospects to agree with a specific vision for Christian education. Schools accpting only students from a specific group within the population of all Christians will be the ones to put forth the greatest effort in recruiting students.

A good example of a school requiring parents to be in agreement with a specific vision is found at Victory Christian School in Tulsa, Oklahoma. The vision of Victory Christian School is more than providing an alternative to the public school; there are other Christian schools in the community with this vision. Their purpose is to have a school where there is prayer, regular Bible reading, strong discipline in the classrooms, a love and appreciation for our nation and heritage, a quality education with degreed teachers and a Bible-based curriculum.

All of these are part of Victory, but this was not the main purpose of the school. What came into the spirit of the founding pastor, Billy Joe Daugherty, was a school to train up students to do the ministry of Jesus. Victory students would be prepared, equipped and trained to take the ministry of Jesus to the ends of the earth.

It is not Victory's expectation to see all students become preachers, pastors, evangelists, prophets, apostles, or teachers; but it expects all of them to be involved in the work of the ministry, whether they are medical professionals, educators, businessmen and women, or in any other vocation.

The Christian School Task

Regardless of the target population and enrollment philosophy, a school will be drawing from students who live in a society where peer pressure and the world of entertainment, movies, music, magazines, television and advertisement are negative influences. In addition, many students enrolling in Christian schools, whether they are Christian kids or not, come out of backgrounds where there has been suspension or expulsion from school; some have tried drugs, alcohol, or tobacco. Others have attended questionable movies and may have participated in unacceptable dating and sexual activities.

Saved and Renewed

Until the non-Christian student is saved, renews his mind with the Word of God and moves toward conforming to Christ-likeness,

Christ-likeness, he will keep making mistakes because of his wrong thinking and inability to "crucify fleshly desires." These may still be dominating him, and his spirit may not be developed to be the dominant factor in his life. What is happening in the lives of students will have an influence on other students, either positive or negative.

Often, Christian schools will exclude students from enrolling and expel others who have obvious conflict in their lives rather than bringing the power of the Word of God, the authority of the believer, and godly wisdom to bear on the situation. It is much easier to remove or exclude students first, rather than confront in love and to be an active change agent in the lives of students.

Perfecting an Army

The task of the Christian school is to grow up and perfect an army of believers capable and able to do the ministry of Jesus. In the process, some soldiers may get off track occasionally; at that point, discipline, correction and a repentance or turning from unacceptable behavior is in order.

Working together with the Church and the Christian home, Christian schools can produce Christian soldiers who will make a difference in this world.

Enrollment Process 2

How can a school determine the number of students who will attend? There is no easy answer to resolving this question. A school must first establish an enrollment goal; then it can refine its enrollment and application processes.

Establish an Enrollment Goal

Whether your school is just beginning its first year of operation, or it has been in existence for several years, you must first determine how many students you expect to enroll. There are some proven strategies to consider.

First Year Schools

Unlike public schools who compute the average percentage of increase/decrease in enrollment over a sequence of grades for a span of time to determine enrollment, first year Christian schools have no previous history upon which to base enrollment projections. Although there is no established formula to calculate first-year enrollment, certain conditions favor a strong first- year enrollment. These include:

1. A strong local economy;
2. Positive community and local church attitude of Christian schools;
3. The past success level of the sponsoring church and strength of existing programs, such as the children's ministry, youth programs and Sunday school;
4. Availability of quality educational facilities;
5. Level of commitment to academic excellence;
6. Zealousness of recruiting efforts.

Letterhead

The Christian school study team has been appointed and is working toward Aug. 26, 1993, as the opening date for our new Christian day school. God has been leading and will continue to lead until the opening of school. We are excited, as many of you are, for the opportunity to establish a Christian day school.

We would like to know your interest in our Christian school by completing this Interest Survey. The information you provide in as indication of interest and involves no obligation or commitment on your part whatsoever.

____ YES, I am interested in the establishment of a Christian Day School.
____ NO, I am not interested at this time.

I am interested in enrolling the following children:

Child 1 Name ______________________________ Age _____ Grade ______
Child 2 Name ______________________________ Age _____ Grade ______
Child 3 Name ______________________________ Age _____ Grade ______

Signature ____

Street Address ____
City ______________________ State ______________ Zip Code ______

Date __________ Telephone Number: Home ______________ Work ______________

We will furnish you with information concerning arrangements for transportation, location and grades to be offered as soon as they are finalized. Continue to pray for wisdom, facilities, faculty, students, curriculum, equipment, transportation, location, promotion and cooperation.

If you have any questions, please call. Use the enclosed envelope to return this survey.

Sincerely,
Pastor

FIGURE 1 - Interest Survey

There are two actions we recommend in identifying enrollment goals for first year schools.

1 Collect first-year enrollment figures from Christian schools located in comparable sized communities and sponsored by ministries of similar size and vision.

2 Conduct a simple interest survey (See Figure 1).

Using good quality letterhead, send the interest survey to as many families as possible, especially those in your own congregation. The responses will provide a list of names of people who you can later recruit to serve on study committees; e.g., such areas as faculty, curriculum, facilities, equipment, finance, transportation, policies and promotion. Enclose a cover letter from the pastor with the interest survey.

Established Schools

Given three to five years of operation, a school could use a linear correlation technique, known as the "least squares" method to predict enrollment. However, this method does not accommodate any variation resulting from external factors, socio-economic change, city expansion, administrative and teacher turnover, relocations to new facilities, improvements in facilities, to name a few.

When Victory Christian School moved from a rented public school facility to a newly constructed modern facility, enrollment was at 835 students. One would expect by moving to a new facility with four activity courts, modern classrooms, new library, computer lab, etc., there would be an automatic increase in enrollment; this was not the case.

Moving the new school about 15 minutes west of the old site, and not having the building completely finished at the time of registration, (because of the commitment to build the school debt free), resulted in a drop in enrollment of 100 students.

The best estimate as to next year's enrollment for an established school, is the present year's enrollment, given all factors remain constant. Any significant change in these factors would influence enrollment. For example, raising tuition 25% for the coming year, moving to another location, or a significant turnover in teaching or administrative staff, will have a negative influence on enrollment. The magnitude of the influence can only be answered by prayer.

All Schools

Prayerfully Seek the Lord

Prayerfully seek the Lord for an enrollment goal. You ask, "Don't you know the Bible says in 1 Corinthians 2:9 '**But as it is written, Eye hath not seen, nor ear heard, neither have entered into the heart of man, the things which God hath prepared for them that love him.**' You can't know how many students to expect."

If you stopped right here and did not read the next verse, you could always plead ignorance. However, the next verse changes the situation. "**But God hath revealed them unto us by his Spirit: for the Spirit searchth all things, yea, even the deep things of God**" (1 Corinthians 2:10).

The Word says "**But ye have an unction from the Holy One, and ye know all things**" (1 John 2:20). All things include the number of students to expect. It is God's desire to reveal this to you. Whether your school is just beginning or it has been established and has a history of enrollment, knowing what God has in mind for enrollment is far more accurate than any mathematical projection.

Act on Your Faith

Through the quickening of the Holy Spirit, you can come to the full realization of an enrollment goal. Once the Spirit impresses upon you the number of students, exercise faith for this goal. Hebrews 11:1 says, "**Now faith is the substance of things hoped for, the evidence of things not seen.**" Putting substance on something in the future is called goal setting.

Once this goal is established, Romans 4:20,21 says to speak out what you believe. Speak forth a supernatural increase in student enrollment. Take action and

1 Begin to declare it so.

> "**For verily I say unto you, That whosoever shall say unto this mountain, Be thou removed, and be thou cast into the sea; and shall not doubt in his heart, but shall believe that those things which he saith shall come to pass; he shall have whatsoever he saith**" (Mark 11:23).

2 Call students in from the north, south, east, and west.

> "**And they shall come from the east, and from the west, and from the north, and from the south, and shall sit down in the kingdom of God**" (Luke 13:29).

3 Command the principalities and powers that are holding students back from enrolling to be removed.

"**For we wrestle not against flesh and blood, but against principalities, against powers, against the rulers of the darkness of this world, against spiritual wickedness in high places** (Ephesians 6:12).

4 Command the blinders to be removed from the eyes of parents so they would see the value of a Christ-centered, Bible-based Christian education for their children.

"...**darkness hath blinded his eyes**" (1 John 2:11).

"...**what fellowship hath righteousness with unrighteousness? and what communion hath light with darkness?**" (2 Corinthians 6:14).

Simplify Application and Enrollment Processes

Don't make your enrollment process so complicated parents and students feel like they are trying to gain admission to Fort Knox. Remember the formula KISS - Keep It Short and Simple. Don't bog parents down with a ton of forms. The simpler the procedures, the more likely parents will enroll their children.

Furthermore, enhance the effectiveness of enrollment by having all school staff, parents and students clearly understand the enrollment (re-enrollment) process.

Prospect Names

As soon as you receive the name of a prospect, take the following steps:

1 Send an information packet containing a letter from the administrator, school brochure, calendar and handbook. The copy of the handbook will help answer questions.

2 Make a follow-up telephone call inviting the student and his family to visit the school.

3 Arrange a tour of the facilities. This is the time to accent all the positive points, such as the gym, swimming pool, modern science lab, typing/computer lab, attractive classrooms, etc. Over the summer, set up one classroom at each division (K-3, 4-6, 7-9, 10-12) as it would look for the first day of school; use this room for visits. Just as a furnished house increases the likelihood of someone making an offer to purchase, a com-

pletely furnished classroom with attractive bulletin boards, displays of children's work, etc., help sell the school.

4 Display your curricula. Have available for inspection various samples of curricula from each grade level. It is worth the initial investment. Parents and students will be impressed by the high quality of Christian curricula. Viewing the textbooks may be the deciding factor for enrolling in your school. Consider a goal of having on display a complete set of the entire school curricula.

5 Provide an opportunity to meet students, teachers and other parents if available at the time of the tour. Treat each prospective family as V.I.P.'s.

Enrollment Packets

Once a decision is made by the parents to seek enrollment, place an enrollment packet in their hands. This packet should contain, as a minimum:

1 A letter from the administrator to the prospective student/family (See Figure 2).

2 A letter from the president of the parent-teacher fellowship.

3 An application form. We recommend your application be a four page panel - 8 1/2" x 11". This provides a natural pocket for inserting enrollment materials.

4 Fee schedule.

5 A listing of the enrollment steps.

6 A sheet of questions and answers.

If finances permit, design a special folder or imprinted envelope for your enrollment packet.

Application Process

The application process needs to be simple, but complete. The following sequence will help:

1 Obtain a completed application for each student enrolled.

2 Review the application.

3 Require at least two letters of reference for students grades 7-12.

LETTERHEAD

(Date)

Dear Parents and Students:

On behalf of the students and staff at (Name of School), I want to welcome you to (Name of School).

In this packet you will find the necessary information to let you become acquainted with our school and to enroll should you choose to attend.

The primary purpose of (Name of School) is to provide a "Quality Education Without Compromising the Word of God." By "Quality Education," we mean creating a school environment in which the fundamental principles of learning are present so students can develop to their fullest potential. Students are taught habits, skills, and attitudes which will allow for great achievement. We seek to develop positive citizens who respect themselves and others, who know how to relate to others, who accept responsibility, possess a sound mind, have strong spiritual values, and who are utilizing their own individual talents, gifts, and abilities to their fullest possible extent.

By not "Compromising the Word of God," we mean God's Word is held high as the student's guide for all learning and development. We encourage Christian growth as outlined in the Scriptures. We intend to teach the Word in such a fashion that our young people will be equipped for service, empowered by the Holy Spirit, and able to use the Word with great authority.

We seek to instill in every student a dependence and trust in God, believing that God is the "Rewarder of all those who diligently seek him."

If you have any questions about our program please feel free to contact us at 432-9199 during office hours (7;30 a.m. - 4:30 p.m).

In His Service,

(Name of Administrator or Pastor)

FIGURE 2 - Prospect Letter

4 Have parents submit an official copy of the child's birth certificate at the time of enrollment.

5 Require a current immunization record. Most state laws require this. This record must be present before acceptance of the application. It is much easier to obtain immunization records at the time of application rather than after school starts.

6 Request payment of a non-refundable enrollment fee along with the application. Return this fee if the applicant is not accepted for admission. Consider a student officially enrolled only after this fee is paid.

7 Arrange for an interview. At the time of the interview, ask for a copy of the student's transcripts and report card. Transcripts are important for the selection of course work.

8 Ask parents and students to read the material explaining the vision of the School. Amos 3:3 speaks of the need to be in agreement if two are to walk together.

"Can two walk together, except they be agreed?"

It only causes confusion when the school is teaching one thing (anti-abortion) and parents believe another (pro-choice); the school teaches that healing and wholeness are for the believer, yet the parents don't believe in healing.

Victory requires parents and family to listen to an audio tape and answer a questionnaire (See Figure 3). Enrollment is only possible if there is agreement with the vision of the school.

Student and Parent Interviews

When students and parents are interviewed, the school views application materials and asks questions to determine whether or not a student should be recommended for admission.

The interviewing process is extremely important, both for the school as well as for parents and students.

Who is Interviewing Who?

When conducting interviews, keep this question in mind; while the school is interviewing the parent and student, they, in turn, are assessing the school. They will pass judgment on the school based on their own impressions during the interviewing session. The way the interviewer dresses, the tone of voice, mannerisms, even how they pray, all contribute to the family's final decision to enroll.

This point was brought home when our daughter took a summer class at another Christian school. While in class, one of the students, who knew our daughter attended Victory, commented, " I was thinking about coming to Victory, but did not come because the person who interviewed us wanted to pray, pray, pray." Praying at the beginning and closing of an interview is a good procedure; after all, prayer should be a vital aspect of

PARENT/STUDENT QUESTIONNAIRE

This questionnaire is to be completed after listening to the Tape, "Our Vision." Completion of the questionnaire is required for enrollment. We recommend parents and students listen to the tape together. Please return this form to the school office as soon as possible.

___Yes ___ No Student - I have listened to the tape titled, "Our Vision."
___Yes ___ No Parent

___ Yes ___ No Student - I am in agreement with the Vision.
___ Yes ___ No Parent

___ Yes ___ No Student - I am regular in chruch attendance.
___ Yes ___ No Parent

___ Yes ___ No Parent - As parents, will you commit to a daily devotional time with your family?

___ Yes ___ No Parent - As a parent will you work with the teachers by assisting your children with their homework, class projects, etc.?

___ Yes ___ No Student - Will you uphold the standards of the school in your home?
___ Yes ___ No Parent

___ Yes ___ No Student - As a student will you uphold the standards of the school both on and off campus?

___ Yes ___ No Student - If there is a conflict, will you resolve differences using the Matthew 18 principle?
___ Yes ___ No Parent

Father's Signature:/ Date: ______________________

Mother's Signature:/ Date: ______________________

Oldest Child: Gr/Date: ______________________
Next Oldest: Gr/ Date: ______________________
Next: Gr/ Date: ______________________
Next: Gr/Date: ______________________
This agreement remains in effect as long as your children are enrolled.

FIGURE 3 - Parent Agreement

any Christian school. How much the interviewer prayed is not known; but according to the perception of this family, too much of a good thing ended up turning the family away.

Interviewing Tips

Some interviewing tips are:

1. Be enthusiastic about the prospects wanting to attend your school.
2. Maintain good eye-to-eye contact.

3 Don't ask questions of obvious information already contained in the application.

4 Don't focus on problems within the school.

5 Avoid being judgmental and condemning.

6 Focus on love, acceptance and forgiveness.

7 Replace pride and arrogance with an attitude of humility and servanthood.

8 Focus on objectives rather than pointing out obstacles.

9 Stress coordination and cooperation rather than independence.

10 Don't cover up mistakes. Focus on people rather than problems.

Respond to Questions

During the interview process, be positive when responding to parents. Listen to the statement they make and respond positively. A list of typical comments, along with suggested, responses follows.

1. ***I don't know where I will enroll my children***. Take the initiative and say, "This school is where they need to be."

2. ***The school work is too difficult.*** God has called us to challenge students to develop to their maximum potential. Have your children developed to their maximum potential in every area of life? Our teachers will help students reach their potential. We want every student to become God's best.

3. ***The school work is too easy.*** Praise God with them for their talent, and encourage them to take advanced classes. They can take honors classes and special study to better prepare for college-entrance testing.

4. ***Our family can't afford it.*** Students cannot afford not to be in a Christian school. Each needs to weigh the value of a good Christian education. Parents will find ways of paying for items they really value. Believe with parents for creative ways to finance the tuition. Remind parents God is their source; believe with them to receive the finances necessary to pay the tuition.

5. ***Not all the students are living a godly life.*** This is the situation at any Christian school and even in a Christian church.

Each student is at a different level of spiritual development. We take students from where they are and help them to grow towards Christ-likeness.

6. ***We have been coming a year, and I can see no changes in my children.*** Change can take place overnight. However, maturing spiritually is a process; it takes time. To see the full effects of a Christian school education, you need to stick with it.

7. ***I cannot get the classes I want.*** Regardless of the school you go to, this will be an issue. It will continue on into college. Final class offerings depend on student enrollment. Our aim is to meet as many needs as we can. Each year, we offer new courses and expand old ones. Courses not offered this semester are offered next semester or next year.

8. ***Discipline is less than adequate.*** The effectiveness of discipline depends on a combination of students, teachers and parents working together on common concerns. Our main concern is helping our students be self-disciplined, mature Christians. As long as students continue to move toward this goal, we will continue to work with them.

9. ***It is too much of a sacrifice.*** God's Word says as parents we are responsible for training our children in the way they should go. This is a command of the Lord. We also know that to obey is better than sacrifice.

10. ***We have no transportation.*** We have school-sponsored transportation. Furthermore, each year we work with families on car pooling. We know from experience, "Where there is a will, there will be a way." When your desire is to do the will of the Father, He reveals a way to enroll your children in school.

11. ***My child isn't learning.*** Much of learning depends on establishing patterns. With some children, this takes time, both time to unlearn old, non-productive patterns, then time to learn new patterns. Children are learning all the time; the rate of growth may be different for different students. We work toward getting our students to believe the Word. It says they were created for good works. We believe good work for students means good grades as indicated in Ephesians 2:10:

"For we are his workmanship, created in Christ Jesus unto good works, which God hath before ordained that we should walk in them."

12. ***How come you have to increase tuition?*** For the Christian school to have the same program next year, it will cost more money. Our school is very competitive in its pricing compared to other schools with similar programs.

13. ***I've heard some bad reports.*** We can resolve 95 percent of the bad reports if persons hearing a bad report would seek clarification. Our increase in student enrollment is not a result of bad reporting, but a result of something good happening.

Thank You

Don't forget the absolutely crucial "Thank You" note. Thank parents and students for considering your school. If they have not made a decision about enrollment, reiterate your interest in wanting their child in school. The Thank You note gives an opportunity to correct any wrong impressions. How many other Christian schools send Thank You notes to those who are considering enrolling in their school? All other factors being equal, the Thank You note may actually attract the student, if not now, later.

Waiting Lists

Be careful when forming waiting lists; they may have an adverse affect on enrollment. For example, suppose your school reaches capacity at a certain grade level and begins a waiting list. Three actions may happen.

First, parents may be very willing to wait around for a position to open. They may begin to pray for an opening by believing for more students necessary to open another section of the particular class with a waiting list. Some parents may even believe for someone to withdraw.

The second case is a parent who, when their children are placed on a waiting list, seeks out another school, enrolls and fails to inform you of this decision. As far as you know, they are still part of your waiting list. Suppose later in the summer, some students already admitted decide to withdraw for financial or other reasons. You immediately call those of your waiting list, only to find out they have already enrolled in other schools. The longer the time a student is on the waiting list, the more likely this will be the case.

A third situation relating to a waiting list occurs when the message circulating becomes, "Your school is already full" when, in fact, it isn't. What may have been at "capacity" for a particular grade, through miscommunication, or rumor, now becomes "no more room in any grade."

In March of 1986, Victory experienced an unusual early response to its re-enrollment campaign. Almost immediately, fourth and fifth grades were filled to capacity.

When enrollment was opened in April to the general public, very few inquiries were received for grades three through six. One day a parent came to inquire about enrolling a first grader. A comment was made during the interview, "We are also considering another school so both of our children can go to the same school." The second child was in sixth grade. The parent was amazed to hear there was still room in our sixth grade; they had heard "our upper elementary grades were already full" and hadn't even considered asking about enrolling in these grades.

This immediately led us to place a few radio and pulpit announcements to get the word out, "There is still plenty of space available." It also prompted us to do away with waiting lists and begin believing God for creative ways to handle all students who wanted to attend.

It is important to consider parents of two or more students where one or more are already enrolled while the others are not enrolled. Experience has shown that these parents are more likely to withdraw their children when room is found for all their children in another school. This may have a ripple effect, especially at the junior and senior high school. If a close friend or relative withdraws to attend another school, there is an increased likelihood, the student already enrolled will also withdraw.

To increase the likelihood of students remaining on waiting lists for admission:

1 Keep in touch with the prospects via phone calls, cards and letters.

2 Notify parents immediately of any openings.

3 Better yet, believe God for creative ways of handling more students.

Admissions Standards

Christian schools have various academic, behavioral and spiritual admission standards. Students must meet these standards to be enrolled. The following suggestions will assist in making quality acceptance and placement decisions.

Academic Standards

Typically, a student is expected to have progressed one grade level academically as measured by a standardized achievement test for each year of schooling. These test results, combined with current academic records from previous schools, provide information necessary to make quality acceptance and placement decisions.

Often, schools admit students only if students can pass an entrance examination. Although some schools have very stringent academic admission standards, most schools admit all students, but maybe not at the expected grade level. For example, a student applies for seventh grade, but because of academic standards, the school accepts him at the sixth grade level.

This type of placement decision is not easy to make. The following strategies may help (See Table 1).

Grades K - 8. Base acceptance in the kindergarten five-year-old program on age; in Oklahoma, a student must be five years old by September 1. A simple kindergarten screening assessment made up of knowledge of letters of the alphabet, understanding of numbers, simple directions, auditory and visual discrimination, listening and speaking vocabulary, along with samples of the completed kindergarten material, will provide the school with information important in making placement decisions.

Grades 9 - 12. Classify students in grades nine through twelve by grade based on completion of credit hours; e.g., X number of credits equals a certain classification, such as freshman, sophomore, junior, or senior; accept students into classes based on successful completion of the subject requirements as identified by a passing grade and credit.

TABLE 1 - Placement Decision Strategies

TEST SCORES	CLASS WORK	DECISON
At or above grade level.	Passing all subject.	Accept at enrolled grade level.
	Failing some subjects.	Accept at enrolled grade level on probation.
One year or more behind grade level in either math or reading.	Passing all subjects.	Accept at grade level, place on probation, be prepared to offer remedial assistance.
	Failing in reading or math.	Accept at previous grade level.
Two or more years below grade level.	Failure in all classes.	Accept at previous grade level only if remedial assistance is available.

Retention Caution. Caution needs to be exercised in retention decisions. Retaining a child at a certain grade does not automatically guarantee the child will be any further ahead at the end of the next year.

Passing from one grade to another; e.g., first to second grade, can be likened to driving a vehicle from Tulsa to Dallas using highway I-44. If a person drives 55 miles per hour, they should make the trip in approximately five hours.

This, of course, assumes there are no detours along the way, the driver doesn't get lost, run out of gas, experience mechanical breakdown and a whole host of other factors.

The same is true of a student in school. He should make it from first to second grade in about nine months, providing there are no complications along the way - death in the family, divorce, loss of pets, teacher turnover, adequate learning processes, prelearning skills, etc.

We know some children experience learning challenges at one time or another; some are able to get back on track, while others need more assistance or more time.

To say to a traveler on his way to Dallas, "I'm sorry, you only made it to Oklahoma City in five hours, so you have to go back to Tulsa and start all over," is like telling a student they will have to repeat a grade.

If, at the end of the school year, it is evident a child has not mastered the necessary skills to go on to the next grade, provide a list of skills yet to be mastered, then assist parents in arranging for the necessary learning experiences during the summer. This may be in the form of summer school, tutors, supplemental textbooks, computer programs, etc.

Other Factors to be Considered

Although standardized achievement scores and present grades are good predictors of future achievement, testimony after testimony has proven the positive effects of a well-disciplined classroom, increased involvement by parents with their child's education and the Christ-centered environment on academic success.

Once students who were poor achievers begin to accept in faith what God's Word says about them and make it part of their school life, they begin to be successful.

For example, in 1 John 5:4-5, we find out students who are born of God, overcome the world.

> **"For whatsoever is born of God overcometh the world; and this is the victory that overcometh the world, even our faith.**
>
> **"Who is he that overcometh the world, but he that believeth that Jesus is the Son of God?"**

School work and studying are part of the student's world, so they can know that God has given them ability to overcome in these areas.

When Christian students fail to realize the "Greater One" resides within them, they become discouraged or even fear receiving a failing grade. By looking at the circumstances, they find themselves speaking words of doubt like, "I can never get the assignment" or, "Brother, I must be stupid" or, "I can't solve this problem. It's too difficult for me." When a student makes statements like these, doubt enters his mind and he fails to realize his potential; he begins to lose his ability to be a success; his faith becomes suppressed.

First John 5:5 says since they believe that Jesus Christ is the Son of God, they will overcome. This belief, coupled with God's promises, gives them God's ability and power to overcome any homework assignment, special project, quiz, nine-week tests, or any other school challenge. Since Jesus is within them, they have the ability of God, wisdom of God and understanding of God, all providing the foundation for school success.

Behavioral and Spiritual Standards

Every school administrator would like to enroll students whose behavior is a strong example of Christ-likeness. However, since only a small percentage of students entering Christian schools for the first time are self-disciplined disciples of Christ, we caution schools not to set their behavioral standards so high they exclude the type of student who could benefit the most from the Christian school.

Spiritual standards are based on the school's enrollment philosophy. As was mentioned earlier, even those students from Christian homes and those who appear to "have it all together" behaviorally and spiritually, may have major challenges in their lives.

Success for enrolling students improves when the following are considered:

1 Establish an environment charged with the love of God where students are loved no matter what, totally accepted as a creation of God; no matter how bad they have fallen, they will be forgiven.

2 Give the Holy Spirit complete freedom. This will lead to conviction (John 16:8) - "**And when he is come, he will reprove the world of sin, and of righteousness, and of judgment,**" and changed lives "**For it is God which worketh in you both to will and to do of his good pleasure**" (Philippians 2:13).

When the Holy Spirit is the chief Admissions Officer, you can have confidence He knows what He is doing and will never allow a person to enter your school who you cannot reach (Acts 13:2; 16:7). The Holy Spirit knows what is in a person (1 Corinthians 2:9-15); He will reveal it to you (Colossians 1:27); and tell you what it takes to see change take place in his/her life (I John 2:20,27).

3 Express concern rather than judgment, forgiveness rather than condemnation.

4 Establish clear standards of conduct. Don't be under the misconception, acceptance breeds automatic approval of inappropriate behavior. Hold students accountable to a prescribed life-style (See Figure 4).

When the school admits students on a foundation of love, acceptance and forgiveness, this will transfer to other students who will, in turn, become able ministers of reconciliation.

Students who are accepted, in turn, will accept themselves and others. This fosters a foundation for boldness and authority, allowing 1 John 4:4 to take on great significance - "**Ye are of God, little children, and have overcome them: because greater is he that is in you, than he that is in the world.**"

Practice Love, Acceptance and Forgiveness

When the full potential of God is released through the operation of the Holy Spirit in a school where love, acceptance and forgiveness flows, achievement will be at its greatest. Students will become successful in everything they put their hands to do.

Students from this type of school will not boast in their own knowledge or wisdom; rather they will boast in the fact they know and understand God.

Schools who practice this philosophy will leave themselves open for misunderstanding; the school may be criticized for emphasizing spiritual development over academic progress. However, when the Word of God is put first place in the school and in the lives of students, the school will be academically successful.

HONOR PLEDGE
(Grades 5-12 - One Per Student)

Students in grades 5-12 will be required to follow the school Code of Conduct personally and sign the honor pledge below.

Recognizing Jesus as the author and finisher of my faith and the Word of God as the supreme standard for all wisdom and knowledge, it is my aim to develop myself accordingly, and to seek His kingdom and righteousness at all times (Hebrews 12:1-2; James 1:5-6; I Peter 1:24; I John 5:3-5).

I will endeavor to follow the will of God for my life and to exemplify Christ-like character through daily personal prayer and consistent study of the Word of God and through faithful group worship both at school and church (Matthew 7:7-11; James 1:22; I Peter 1:13-16; I John 2:5-6).

I will apply myself to my studies and endeavor to develop the full powers of my mind in Christ (Luke 2:52; Phil. 2:5; I Cor. 1:5).

I will practice good health habits and regularly participate in wholesome physical activities (I Cor. 3:16-17; Romans 12:1).

I will yield my personality to the Holy Spirit (James 5:14-16; Acts 1:8; Acts 2:1-4).

I will endeavor to faithfully give heed to the call of God on my life and develop the gifts and abilities God has given me (I John 2:20; I Cor. 12:18-31; Ephesians 4:11-12).

I will seek to practically share the love of God through personal witness and specific ministry on a regular basis in an area of Christian service where I feel led/called (Matt. 28:19-21; 10:8; John 15:17; I cor. 15:58; II Cor. 5:18; I Cor. 9;22).

I will submit myself to the leadership of the school and any rules or regulations that may be adopted or changed from time to time. I realize that my attendance here at school is a privilege and not a right. I determine to give my best and to prayerfully support the school staff and its philosophy of providing a quality education without compromising the Word of God. This pledge will become part of my permanent file.

Student's Signature   Grade   Date

Parent's Signature   Grade   Date

Which item do you sense will take the greatest effort on your part? Why?

Figure 4 - Student Honor Code

Parent Notification

It is important to make acceptance decisions as soon as possible. Admission decisions should be made by an admissions team. This team may be composed of any number of individuals - headmaster, principal, teacher, parent leaders, pastor, chaplain, or counselor - but no fewer than three. The importance in a team approach is:

1 In the safety of a multitude of counselors,
2 Providing a more thorough and objective assessment of the applicant, and
3 Removing any single person from making an admissions decision, thereby avoiding the "bad guy" label often given to the bearer of bad news.

Make each decision after prayerful consideration. Often, there will be a positive confirmation or inner witness directly following the interview. When this happens, it is best to communicate your acceptance or rejection after the interview and followup with an official letter.

Regardless of the decision:

1 Notify parents in writing no more than ten working days following the interview.
2 Display a tender, caring concern rather than making judgmental statements. Even though a student has been rejected, they need to feel you care about them.
3 If warranted, offer an opportunity for the applicant to reapply at a later date. Keep this information on hand for future followup.

Provide an environment where academic success can be a natual outgrowth of the supernatural inner growth of the very life and presence of God.

Marketing and Media

3

Effective use of marketing and media strategies will keep your school before the community. Employing the strategies suggested in this chapter will help your school pass "the man on the street test."

Go downtown or to the busiest place in town. Stop 100 people and ask them to give you names of Christian schools in the community. If one person names your school, it passes the test.

Everyone knows marketing is important in building a business. It turned hamburger stands into international chains. It has turned soft drinks into billion-dollar industries. Marketing isn't just for businesses; it's for any organization wanting to set their sights high and get where they want to go.

Develop a School Brochure

A quality brochure is an absolute must for any Christian school wanting to gain positive exposure in their community. The school brochure is a key recruiting tool. Place it in every information packet, on every display table and in every school mailing.

Elements of a quality brochure include:

1. Using good quality pictures - students prefer to see photos of good looking, smiling, fun-loving students rather than photos of students thinking and studying.
2. Stating your purpose and vision in simple and to the point language.
3. Placing addresses and phone numbers.
4. Stressing variety.
5. Accenting quality.

6 Mentioning sports program and student activities - as many as 80 percent of your students will participate in some form of sport or activity.

7 Using four-part color is more expensive; however, four-part color brochures are far more effective than those done in one or two colors.

Develop Special Brochures

As your school develops and you have an outstanding faculty, you may want to emphasize this in a special brochure. Consider using a special brochure accenting your spiritual and academic focus, missions and community service opportunities. Highlight your fine and performing arts programs.

Inform Other Churches in Your Community

"Reaching the pastors in your community takes more time and effort than advertising through the mass media, but the church-going students and families they represent are worth the time invested" (White and Enderlin, 1986).

Send a personal letter (See Figure 5) to pastors of churches who would agree with your vision, goals, or purposes. Followup by arranging a personal contact with as many pastors as possible. Prepare to:

- Meet with them in a restaurant at your school's expense.
- Provide copies of your school brochure and other Christian school promotional material.
- Deal with the issue of proselytism. If you offer tuition discounts only to members of your church, explain your intentions and assure them it is not to recruit members from other churches.
- Seek support of the pastors by their willingness to promote your school in their churches both from the pulpit and by making promotional fliers available.

Provide a senior pastor discount to those pastors who agree with the vision and stated purpose of the school. This will result in a greater willingness to promote your school (See Appendix A - Senior Pastor Discount).

LETTERHEAD

Dear Pastor:

It is a privilege to be fellow laborers with you in the Kingdom of God. We know that whatever we can do to help each other to better equip the saints is fulfilling the exhortation of Psalm 133:1, "Behold, how good and how pleasant it is for brethren to dwell together in unity."

With this in mind, we would like to offer our assistance in sharing the ministry of (Name of School) with you and your body of believers. We believe that you, too, are committed to quality education without compromising the Word of God.

Selected people from our staff will be available upon your invitation to set up a display, and/or answer questions. We will be calling you soon for your advisement. Thank you for your kind consideration and help. If you have any questions, please contact us at 254-8626.

We appreciate you and your ministry.

"Train up a child in the way he should go: and when he is old, he will not depart from it" (Prov. 22:6).

In His Love and Service,
Pastor or Administrator

FIGURE 5 - Pastor Letter

Develop a First Response Piece

Many of your recruiting strategies will result in an inquiry about the school. When this happens, the person moves from being a prospect to being a candidate for enrollment.

You need an attractive first response piece to place in their hands. This may be a school brochure, information packet, or letter from the headmaster.

Develop Public Awareness

Public awareness can be accomplished using a bulk mail flier, mass coverage of select neighborhoods with door hangers, mass media advertising in the newspaper, radio and television and news releases.

Bulk Mailing

In communicating to the public by using a bulk mailer, consider the following pointers:

1 **Identify the size of your mailing**. Will you mail to all private homes in specified zip codes, or in a four to eight mile radius of your school?

2 **Determine the number of mailings**. The number of mailings relates directly to the cost. We recommend two mailings, one sent in early April when parents are beginning to think about the effectiveness of the present school term, and a second mailing the first week in August when parents are thinking about the coming school term.

3 **Investigate bulk rates**. Contact your local post office and mailing services for specific guidelines on bulk mailing. It is possible to save as much as 30 percent - 40 percent by using special mailing rates and services.

4 **Secure permits**. Arrange for a bulk mailing permit or use your church's bulk mail permit.

5 **Obtain professional help in designing your flier**. A well-designed flier is a good communicator. Clear information is easy to understand and read.

   We recommend a four-panel pamphlet. Panel 1 is the first to be seen; therefore, it should attract attention and tell the reader what the pamphlet contains; Panel 2 leads the reader into the main message about your school; Panel 3 is the inside section containing the key information about the school. Print the information across the panel so the reader does not have to turn the pamphlet on its side to read it; Panel 4 is for addressing.

6 **Print enough copies**. In designing your brochures, fliers, or other items, try not to include "time-dated" information. This will allow printing of more copies and reduce your overall per piece printing cost.

7 **Include vital data**. Insure the mailer includes the address of the school and both a daytime and an after 5 p.m. telephone number.

8 **Attach a response card.** Design a response card (or section) for use in all bulk mailings. This could take the form of an insert or panel to be torn off and returned to the school. Designing response cards with the school address and postage (Permit) will increase the likelihood of a response (See Figure 6).

NO POSTAGE NECESSARY IF MAILED IN THE UNITED STATES

ATTENTION VICTORY CHRISTIAN SCHOOL

BUSINESS REPLY MAIL
FIRST CLASS PERMIT NO. 8188 TULSA, OK
POSTAGE WILL BE PAID BY ADDRESSEE

Victory Christian Center
7370 EAST 71st STREET
TULSA, OKLAHOMA 74133

☐ YES, PLEASE FORWARD INFORMATION ON VICTORY CHRISTIAN SCHOOL.

Name______________________________

Address______________________________

City____________ State______ Zip______

☐ YES, I WOULD LIKE A CALL FROM THE SCHOOL.

Phone______ ________________
(area code)

"TRAIN UP A CHILD IN THE WAY HE SHOULD GO: AND WHEN HE IS OLD, HE WILL NOT DEPART FROM IT."
Proverbs 22:6

FIGURE 6 - Response Card

Mass Media Advertising

Radio and Television

Radio reaches 88 percent of Americans at home every week. Ninety-three percent of those who commute to work listen to the radio while commuting, 85 percent listen while shopping for groceries, 91 percent while retail shopping, and 88 percent while dining out.

There are two advantages of using radio and television advertising for recruiting students.

First, the school can appeal to a very large audience in a very short time. The stations you select should be those watched most often by your target group. Don't assume the only stations Christian parents and students listen to or watch are Christian stations.

Second, you can reach and attract prospects who are not actually considering enrolling in a Christian school.

The following strategies are important.

1 Write to your radio and television stations requesting information for potential advertisers, including detailed information on the number of persons who listen and their characteristics.

2 Make a point to visit the station; meet the people who prepare the news and ads.

3 Speak with the broadcasters, and seek the kinds of information they would like for the community.

4 Get back to them with a news item or ad when your name is still fresh in their mind.

5 Your goal is to establish a professional relationship that is mutually respectful.

6 Tackle radio and television advertising only if you are willing to make a financial and time commitment towards quality.

Community Calendar

Contact your area radio stations to see if they conduct a "Community Calendar" or radio bulletin board to announce upcoming community events. These programs usually have a large listening audience. This is an excellent avenue for getting news of your school out into the community, and they are usually free. Generally, all it takes is the information placed on a 3" x 5" index card.

Rotating Announcements

Most schools, when they purchase radio air time, focus on one single message repeated over and over. Rather than playing six spots, if the same message, consider rotating six different spots. Design each spot to focus on a different aspect of the school. The lead into the announcement and the closing are similar (See Figure 7).

On-the-Spot Coverage

Many times radio stations will broadcast from various locations in the community. Accomplish this in conjunction with an open house. Make spot announcements throughout the programming, inviting the community to visit the Christian school.

Christian Radio

Encourage Christian radio stations to be supportive of Christian education. To show their support:

1 Encourage them to run spots between May and September to help educate their audience about Christian education.

2 Rotate the spots once every hour between 6:00 a.m. and 6:00 p.m., Monday through Saturday.

3 Suggest the station provide a special rate to Christian schools to run spots of their school following the educational spots.

4 Offer to write the script for the educational spots in exchange for some free spots featuring your school.

A sample of some spots produced for KCFO in Tulsa, Oklahoma, is found in Appendix B. The material was developed from literature produced by Paul Kienel and Roy Lowrie.

TV Footage and Special Issues

Invite TV stations to use your school and students when the station needs footage for educational issues, such as "prayer in the schools." In addition, whenever you are going to have a special event, let the media know.

Special Spots

When a sponsoring church has a radio or TV program, add school spot announcements at the end of the program. These spots can be produced at very little extra cost.

As with all radio and television announcements, select someone to do the dialogue who has a "golden voice."

Focus - Early Childhood Education. Since 1979, Victory Christian School has provided a quality early childhood program, with more than 600 students graduating from its five-year-old kindergarten class. Victory's early childhood program, Reading, Arithmetic, Phonics, Science, Writing and Bible, build a solid base for entry into elementary school. Along with Victory's Enrichment program, children have the opportunity for a full day time of learning and having fun. For more information about Victory's early childhood program, ages 4-5, call 254-8626. That's Victory Christian School, 254-8626, providing quality education without compromising the Word of God.

Focus - Family Involvement. Since 1979, Victory Christian School has been a leader in establishing a successful elementary program during the most impressionable periods of a child's life. Victory's certified faculty cooperate with parents and guardians in building a strong foundation during these formative years. Programs in physical education, swimming, art and music, taught by special teachers, add to the enjoyment of strong academics. For more information about Victory Christian School, call 254-8626. That's 254-8626...Victory Christian School - a leader in quality Christian education.

Focus - Junior High. Since 1979, Victory Christian School has specially planned for the time of transition from elementary to middle or junior high school. Along with a well-balanced academic program, there is development of the student's self-image and an understanding of what they can achieve in life as they commit their abilities to becoming their very best in whatever they put their hand to do. Victory's junior high program builds on a strong elementary foundation and prepares the student for a successful senior high experience. For a visit to our school site or information packet, call Victory Christian School, 254-8626. That's 254-8626...Victory Christian School - a leader in quality Christian education.

Focus - Post High School Study. Since 1979, Victory Christian School has had graduating students that have been taught the qualities of life from a spiritual and an academic viewpoint. Graduates are equipped for the college of their choice or to enter their respective careers. Victory Christian School graduates have been accepted at Colleges, Universities, Vocational Schools and Bible Schools, such as ORU, Evangel College, TU, Florida State, Washington State, TJC, University of Arkansas, OU, and West Point - to name a few. VCS is accredited through the International Christian Accrediting Association and the Oklahoma State Department of Education. It is never too late to make the change to Victory Christian School, call 254-8626. That's 254-8626...Victory Christian School - a leader in quality Christian education.

Focus - Spiritual. Since 1979, Victory Christian School students have been trained to trust in the Lord with all their heart and not to lean unto their own understanding, to acknowledge Him in all their ways, and to have their paths directed by Jesus Christ. Victory Christian School students have seen God's Word confirmed in their lives with signs following. Salvation, Healing, and Miracles are a way of life with students at Victory Christian School - a leader in quality Christian education.

Focus - Facilities. Since 1979, Victory Christian School has been building strong families. Parents can have confidence in Victory's commitment to a student lifestyle that fosters harmony in the home, respect for authority, and builds strong moral character. Victory Christian School staff are dedicated to helping parents successfully meet the challenges presented by today's youth. For a copy of the Victory Christian School student handbook and information packet, call 254-8626.

FIGURE 7 - Rotating Radio Spots

Radio Public Service Announcements

Most radio stations accept written public service announcements. The most popular are 10- and 15-second spots. A good rule of thumb in writing a script is about 25 words fit in ten seconds and 50 in fifteen seconds. Expect a two-week delay time before the announcement airs. It costs very little - just paper, envelopes and stamps. Followup with a "thank you" note when you get on the air.

Television Public Service Announcements

Local networks and cable stations offer public service announcements. Before investing time and funds, call the cable stations and find out what the possibilities are of getting on the air. The best announcements are ones that look like real commercials.

Focus your PSA spot on an answer to a pressing local or national issue - "Latch Key Children," "Teenage Rebellion," or "AIDS Education." Conclude the spot with: "This message is brought to you by VICTORY CHRISTIAN SCHOOL - Quality without compromise." Do everything you can to produce a quality spot.

For assistance in producing quality low-cost spots, contact: Video Impact, 807 South Xanthus Place, Tulsa, Oklahoma 74104 (918-582-4464).

Talk Shows

An opportunity may be available to present your view on a local radio, network, or cable television. Determine why you should be on the program; then give the producer of the show a call. Before going on the air, write down ahead of time three to five points you want to make, and be sure to say them no matter what you are asked. The popularity of the show will determine your impact.

Published Resources

A simple booklet titled, *If You Want Air Time* (National Association of Broadcasters, 1985), provides useful do's and don'ts for getting the most out of local radio and television outlets. This resource contains advice for using radio and television stations, along with detailed information about station requirements.

Press Release

Most newspaper and radio stations accept a well-written press release about the opening of a new Christian school in the community. For existing schools, any substantial changes in staffing, facilities, or programs are well received. Stations often accept announcements of classes, workshops, conferences, and special events. The following guidelines will increase the likelihood of acceptance of your releases by the station:

1 On the first page of the copy, type your name, address, phone number, brief description of the subject matter, number of words and who will receive the release (See Figure 8).

2 Since very few editors have the time to read the entire release, keep the important facts close to the beginning. Another reason is headline writers get their headlines from the lead paragraph.

3 Keep the release simple and concise. Construct sentences 15-20 words long and paragraphs about 75 words.

4 Use an effective lead sentence. A good "grabber" will catch the attention of the readers and establish interest to continue reading. For example, Abundant Life Christian School in Madison, Wisconsin, informed the newspaper they were going to go after the Guinness Book of World Records for a paper chain.

Upon the completion of the chain, what do you think was on the front cover of the newspaper? You're right - an eight-by-eleven inch color picture of the paper chain, along with hundreds of smiling faces, the name of the school in big headlines and a brief caption. The news release stated: Abundant Life Christian School goes for Guinness Book of World Records. The final newspaper copy read: "CHAIN OF LOVE. You could call this a chain gang, but here love is the chain that binds. The students of Abundant Life Christian School, 4909 E. Buckeye Road, have made more than 1,500 feet of paper chain. The students plan to continue work on the chain, hoping to reach 4,000 feet and a world record."

DATE

Name of institution

Public relations department

Contact: (Name of spokesman or person handling the information)

Release: (Immediate - or time the news agency may release the information)

Address:__________Zip:______

Telephone: __________ Area Code:______

Use this space for any special instructions to the editor.

____

____

____

____

Dateline (city from which story originated) - (Special) - THE LEAD

PARAGRAPH is the "Grabber" - catching the attention of the reader and establishing interest to continue reading. It tells what the following copy is about.

Design The BODY COPY to develop facts of the story. It is important that the "GUTS" of the story be told first. Very few editors have the time to read the entire release, so get the important facts close to the beginning.

Another reason: Remember, writers get their headlines from the lead paragraphs.

FIGURE 8 - Press Release

5 State the facts clearly and concisely. Be accurate. Don't take the word of others. It is embarrassing to be wrong.

6 Always tell the truth. Experts read these releases. They can spot a "PHONY" a mile away.

7 Type the copy on letter-size paper using double spacing, one and one half inch margins. If you must use more than one page, put <u>more</u> at the bottom of each - except the last, where you place the end symbol - #.

8 Have several individuals proofread the release.

9 Hand carry the release whenever possible.

10 After the release, follow-up with a phone call or thank you letter. Good rapport developed early in the history of the school will pay off in assuring fair and interested handling of the school's future request for media coverage.

11 Believe God. Christian schools need to believe God for supernatural advertising and creative ways to bring this about.

Other Mass Media Considerations

There are probably several newspapers circulating in your community; some communities have more than one newspaper. Large metro areas may also have several suburban papers. Small towns are likely to have a daily or weekly paper. Additional papers, such as "shoppers," may be circulating as well as "recreational" or "seasonal" newspapers. Your focus should be those newspapers serving the community your school wants to reach with its message.

By writing to the newspapers of interest, you can obtain advertising rates, additional information about circulation, procedures and deadlines for submitting advertisement and editorials.

When placing church ads, drop a one-line reference to your school in the bottom right-hand corner of your ad.

Religious and Educational Editorials

Newspapers invite community response to religious and educational issues. If you have a strong opinion on an issue or are misrepresented:

- Write your newspaper.
- Think through your response.
- Write it well.
- Make a phone call first, and prepare to send information right away if you get a positive response.

News Stories and Articles

Many times a newspaper editor is looking for an article with just the right amount of space to complete a full page. Yours may be the one selected! Timely, interesting, or new items are news worthy.

Smaller cities are very receptive to accepting articles and news stories from private schools. It takes a little more PR to get them accepted in large cities. Begin by getting to know the religious editor.

Letters

A letter to an editor is one of the fastest ways of getting something into print when the letter is:

- Brief.
- Thoughtful.
- Able to hold the reader's attention.
- Presented in a timely fashion.

Watch carefully the impression it will leave upon the community.

Columns

Watch columns in various papers, and note the types of information presented. Submit information of interest for inclusion in a column.

A column might be a simple listing of facts that happened 5, 10, or 20 years ago. Use your school newspapers, yearbooks, or historical log to compile items for these listings.

Art work

Newspaper editors are always looking for charts, graphs, maps and other line illustrations, as well as photographs.

Consider submitting some of these from your school; include student art.

Published Articles

Well-written articles for community, denominational or national publications are good positioning tools. Copy these articles, and use them as promotional pieces.

A good article for fall would be one titled, "Back-to-School Shopping."

General Advertising

Be creative in the placement of your advertisements. Pictures or illustrations are far more effective than just words (See Figure 9).

FIGURE 9 - General Advertisement

Outdoor Advertising

Advertise your school on billboards throughout your community.

1 Check with individual companies for rate and availability.
2 Don't wait until the very last minute to secure billboard space. Many times there may be a three to four month turnaround time.
3 Personally go out and view each recommended location.
4 Get a good design, and use no more than eight words or a picture board if possible.
5 Consider erecting your own billboards on property owned by the church, parents and friends of the school.
6 Contact vendors with marquees to display special messages for special events; e.g., "Congratulations to Victory Christian School - City Spelling Champions," "Welcome back to school - Victory Christian School," "Good job, Victory Christian School winners of Tri-State Basketball," etc.

Card Signs on Buses

Messages used for card signs on buses must be brief and to the point. Phone numbers are useless; most people who see the sign do not have pencil and paper to write down the number, or time to read and remember the numbers.

Use pictures and no more than eight words. You are looking for attention getters at a glance.

Sign on Property

Erect a sign stating, "Enrollment is now open" on your school property. If your sponsor church already has a marquee, add a line or two at the bottom of the marquee.

Yellow Pages and Coupons

Check your yellow pages to see how your school name is listed. Adding large print or a special box will attract more attention. If it results in enrolling one additional student, it will be worth the extra cost. Enter your school name in as many directories as possible. Remember - exposure, exposure, exposure.

Place a coupon in a community coupon packet. It is possible to reach a large group of homes for a fraction of the cost of doing your own mailing (See Figure 10.)

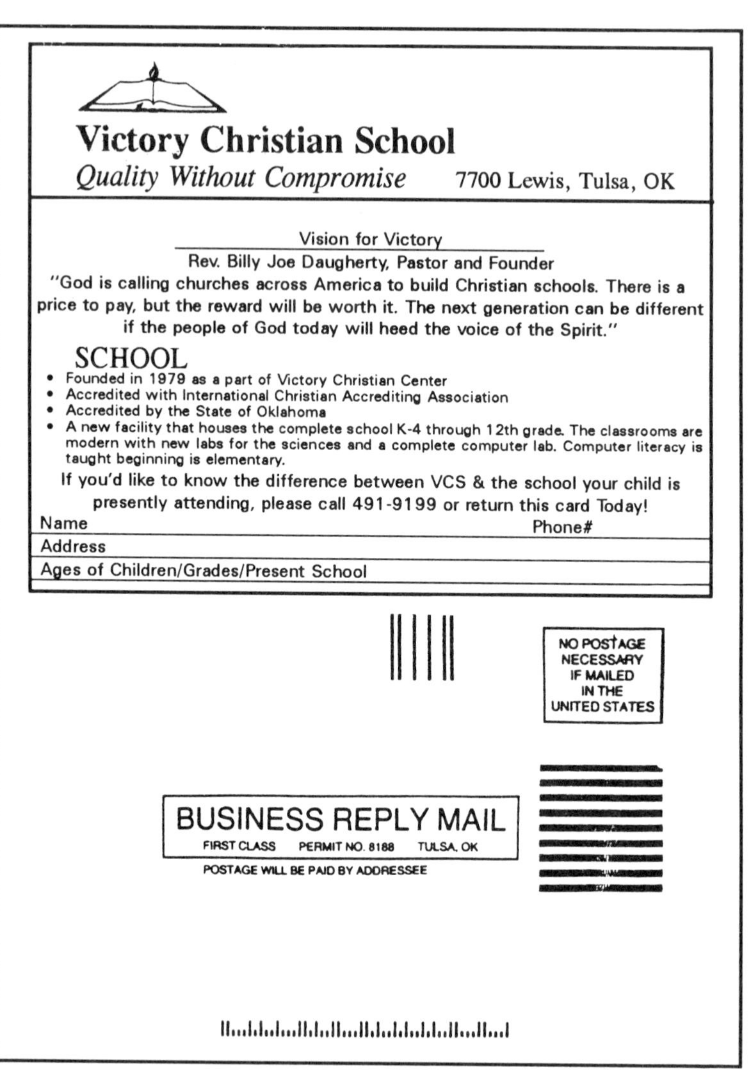
Victory Christian School
Quality Without Compromise 7700 Lewis, Tulsa, OK

Vision for Victory
Rev. Billy Joe Daugherty, Pastor and Founder
"God is calling churches across America to build Christian schools. There is a price to pay, but the reward will be worth it. The next generation can be different if the people of God today will heed the voice of the Spirit."

SCHOOL
- Founded in 1979 as a part of Victory Christian Center
- Accredited with International Christian Accrediting Association
- Accredited by the State of Oklahoma
- A new facility that houses the complete school K-4 through 12th grade. The classrooms are modern with new labs for the sciences and a complete computer lab. Computer literacy is taught beginning is elementary.

If you'd like to know the difference between VCS & the school your child is presently attending, please call 491-9199 or return this card Today!

Name Phone#
Address
Ages of Children/Grades/Present School

NO POSTAGE NECESSARY IF MAILED IN THE UNITED STATES

BUSINESS REPLY MAIL
FIRST CLASS PERMIT NO. 8188 TULSA, OK
POSTAGE WILL BE PAID BY ADDRESSEE

FIGURE 10 - Coupon

Telephone Time and Temperature

Many cities have a special number to call to obtain the time and temperature. Prior to giving the time and temperature, the message tells the organization that is sponsoring the call. For example, "This message is brought to you by Victory Christian

School - it is not too late to enroll for this new school term." The message is followed by the time and temperature. In many cases these announcements are free to non-profit organizations or are offered at a reduced rate.

Promotional Posters

Arrange to have a colorful poster printed and displayed in the windows of businesses in your community - start with your vendors. Ask parents to place posters where they work. Location is critical. Consider barber shops, beauty shops, doctor's offices, dentist's offices, clinics, bus stops, laundromats, bulletin boards in grocery and drug stores, places of employment, skyways, etc.

Bumper Stickers and License Plates

Don't overlook the power of bumper stickers to expose your school. Give a free bumper sticker to every family enrolling - "My Children Attend Victory Christian School - Quality Without Compromise." Give bumper stickers to parents of honor roll students - "My Son (Daughter) Is an Honor Student at Victory Christian School." The messages available for bumper stickers are limitless. Be creative with your messages. Place the name of your school on all bumper stickers.

In some states not requiring license plates on the front of vehicles, create an attractive school plate. A quality plate may last five to eight years.

Air Display

Contact the local airport and find out who is available to do aerodisplays. The name of your school flown behind an airplane provides unique exposure, and given the right timing, may be obtained at very little cost to non-profit organizations.

Paper Products

Contact the pizza or other fast food outlets near your school; arrange to have your school name and logo placed on drinking cups. Victory Christian School was able to place its name on refill cups at one of Tulsa's frequently attended pizza places.

Many times, a school is able to have its name placed on grocery sacks for very little cost.

City Maps

An area often overlooked for advertising is on city-wide maps. Contact advertising agencies as well as map makers for prices and circulation. Calvary Academy has been very successful in placing its school name on the Fort Worth city map (See Figure 11).

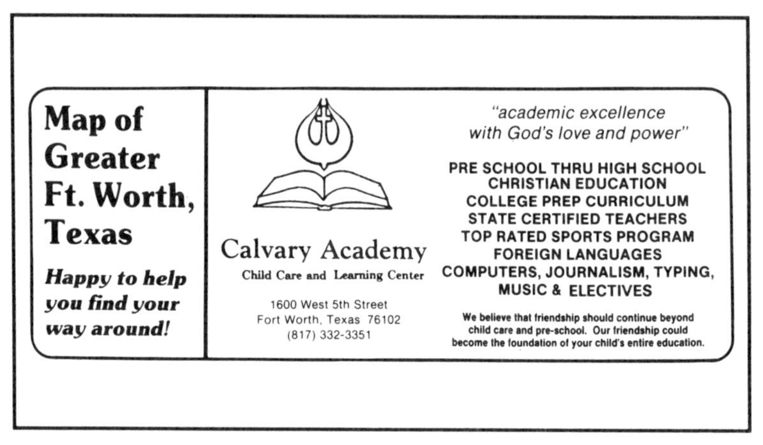

FIGURE 11 - City Map

Special Events

Invite the news media to special events, such as concerts, dramas, parent workshops, chapels, spelling bees, kite day and graduation; provide free passes to sporting events.

Consider the following pointers for publicizing an event.

1 Pick a type of event that no one is doing. If there have been three walk-a-thons this spring, you'll have a difficult time garnering exposure.

2 Choose the location as carefully as you would choose your own neighborhood. Can people get there? Will they want to go there?

3 Everything takes longer than you think. Be generous in allocating time on the project.

4 Pick a day you're reasonably certain that a competing event will not occur. Parades, carnivals and other public gatherings must obtain permission from the municipality. Check with City Hall.

5 The more commercial the event, the more innovative it must be to warrant coverage. The press may be generous with worthy causes, but spectacles staged to sell soap have to offer a promise of novelty.

6 Start way ahead of time in getting the required permissions from the community.

For more suggestions on getting press coverage see William Parkhurst, *How to Get Publicity* (1985).

Presentations and Performances

Arrange for school presentations and performances at sporting events, shopping malls, city parks, or conventions. Consider using choir, band, gymnastics, drama, art productions, spelling bee, Bible bowls, quiz teams, rope jumpers, etc..

Displays

Shopping centers, conventions, bank lobbies, airports, train stations, public libraries and health clubs are some good places for displays. When such opportunities occur, you will find it useful to have a portable display that is easy to adapt to the nature of the event.

You can invest in a quality display for use during special events; place it on display in your school between events. Standard display kits purchased from professional display vendors have the best results, although local craftsmen can make a custom design to your specifications. The intent of the display is to create an interest in your school and lead people to request more information.

Keep the display up to date and fresh looking. Use lots of pictures.

Audio-Visual

More schools are employing audio-visual and video media to supplement recruiting literature. These may range from a brief slide show to sophisticated videotape presentations aired on TV, to ones presented before and after church services, set up at information tables, or viewed at the convenience of interested students and parents.

Video tapes have important benefits: they enable prospective families to view the school in action and listen to students, parents and school staff discuss their experiences, responsibilities and reactions to school.

Ideally, all audio-visual materials should supplement and reinforce other information contained in your recruiting literature.

Academic Tests

You can be especially effective in attracting students by placing a newspaper advertisement in a test format. Construct a series of math and reading questions based on the end-of-year kindergarten curriculum if your target group is kindergarten children. Ask parents to have their children take the test mentioned below. At the conclusion, make some statement such as, "How well did your child do? All kindergarten children at Victory Christian School were able pass this test! For more information on how your child can receive a quality academic education, call 491-9199."

Training

Since most schools produce their own recruiting materials, attending workshops on layout, design and desk-top publishing enhance the school's ability to produce quality-written materials - brochures, newsletters, direct mail, etc. The workshops may be expensive, but are worth the investment of both time and money.

Networking

Network marketing is the hottest technique used today in direct sales. Fortune 500 companies are using network marketing to reach consumers face to face.

Through network marketing, Christian schools can get many people involved in promoting the school.

1. Ask board members, staff, students, parents and friends to convey your school message.
2. See that every pastor and Sunday school teacher has information packets about the school.
3. Ask everyone you know to introduce you to likely prospects. Every parent who enrolls knows at least five other families whose children could benefit from attending a Christian

school. People respond best to initial contacts from people they know. Even if a person in not interested in the school, ask for a referral of someone they know who would be interested. Have special referral cards designed for this purpose (See Figure 12).

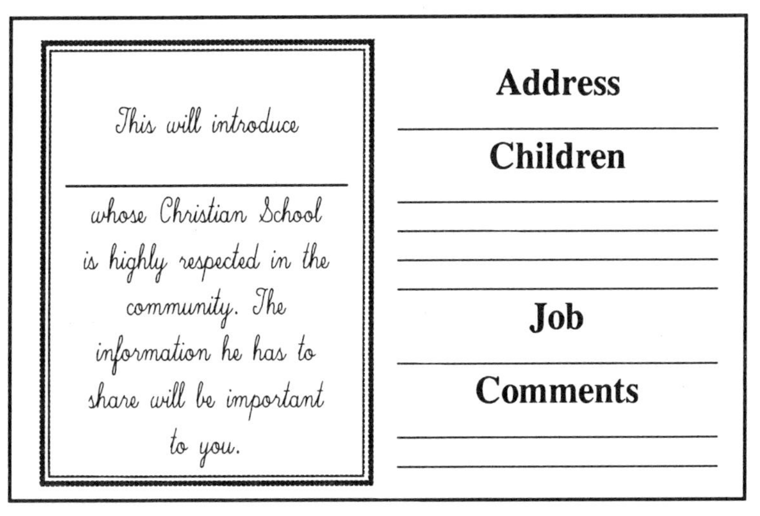

This will introduce

____

whose Christian School is highly respected in the community. The information he has to share will be important to you.

Address

____

Children

____

____

____

____

Job

____

Comments

____

____

FIGURE 12 - Referral Card

Deal with Criticism

Whether your school is just starting or it is an established school, you will have to deal with criticism. T.L. Osborn said, "Men and women who get ideas and get things done are always criticized. Critics always dog the train of achievers . . . People only criticize the man out front. The frail person, the non-successful person, the orthodox run-of-the mill person commands no attention."

The more exposure your school receives, the greater the risk of criticism. This criticism may focus on any aspect of the school. It may come from within the Christian school community or from the outside. Regardless of the source of criticism, handling criticism effectively will significantly affect the success of the total recruitment efforts.

The responsibility of answering criticism must be taken by the school leadership, ideally the headmaster or superintendent. Give one person responsibility for answering criticism. This allows for more effective responses and better control.

Thus, everyone fielding criticism should refer to the spokesperson designated to answer criticism. Having a single spokesperson respond to all criticism will result in greater consistency. This, in turn, helps build greater credibility. Criticism answered consistently, thoroughly without evasions and misleading vagueness, and in a timely fashion, causes the critic (press, community leader, parents, etc.) to accept or recognize the validity of the school's position or action.

Don't Reinvent the Wheel

Borrowing ideas and materials from other schools and businesses can result in a substantial savings of time and finances. Schools with limited financial resources to employ professional designers and writers can look for ways to adapt or modify promotional ideas and materials from businesses and corporations. Keep a watchful eye for current advertising and design trends.

Every Christian school must be able to pass the "Man-on-the-street test."

4

Other Recruiting Strategies

The first target group is your "warm" market. These are individuals who are already familiar with your school, the church, or group of churches sponsoring the school. Since these people already know about the school and church, they will be more receptive at listening to what you have to say.

Recruit Families From Your Church

The first group to consider is families who attend the sponsoring church or churches. These are the ones who will be the most familiar with your school. It is to this group you need to effectively communicate the vision of your Christian school. Don't assume that just because they attend your church, they are familiar with your school. The following strategies have proven to be effective in recruiting students from local churches.

Active Leaders

Recruiting efforts need to focus on the entire church congregation. However, parents already actively involved in a church need to be your first concern. These should receive a personal invitation to enroll their children; include ushers, greeters, Sunday School teachers, bus ministry workers, children's church workers, and any others involved in any aspect of the church or churches.

Sunday School Classes

The Sunday school of the sponsoring church provides an immediate population of potential students. Develop and distribute to Sunday school classes promotional materials written for various age groupings; e.g., kindergarten, first - third, fourth - sixth, junior high and senior high. Consider the following letter written

(Letterhead)

Dear Parents,

Thank you for your interest in our Kindergarten. We are praying that you and your child will be blessed during this special time in his/her life. We feel a child's first experiences in school are extremely important and set the tone for all the school years that follow. When a child has a happy and secure experience at school, he/she will be able to learn and grow in all areas of their spirit, soul, and body. In our K-4 and K-5 classes, we love to learn, and we have fun while we learn.

The following is a little information taken from our Kindergarten handbook to give you an idea of what we do. We use the Bob Jones Kindergarten curriculum for basic lessons, and we hold school 5 days a week for 3 hours; AM (8:10-11:00) and PM (12:10-3:00). If you have any more questions, please feel free to contact us at school.

Here are just a few of the special things we do:

1. We learn about God's Word.
2. We memorize parts of God's Word.
3. We learn to pray and praise the Lord.
4. We practice walking in the fruit of the Spirit.
5. We learn about all the letters and sounds they make.
6. We learn to count and recognize numbers.
7. We practice cooking with special kindergarten recipes.
8. We learn about the world God made in science.
9. We learn about colors and shapes in art.
10. And in K-5 we learn to read and to add and subtract.

We also have an enrichment program in the afternoon, so that mothers who work would be able to have a secure place for their children all day.

We are very happy with the program God has provided at (Name of School), a program that parents can have confidence in and children can achieve their maximum potential.

We are looking forward to a very special time of graduation for each K-5 student and a special welcome into first grade. Would you consider (Name of School) for next year? You and your family will be blessed.

In His Service,

Early Childhood Coordinator

FIGURE 13 - Sunday School Preschool Letter

by a kindergarten teacher to parents who have children in the Sunday school preschool department (See Figure 13).

Bulletin Inserts

Place in your church bulletin a series of unique one- to two-page reports to the congregation about different aspects of the school. Focus on special concerns parents and students might have about enrolling in a Christian school, such as: The Christian School Curriculum: How It Benefits Students, Parents and Teachers; Christian Education: More Than An Option; Reasons For Sending Your Child To A Christian School; Is a Christian Education Worth the Financial Investment? Christian School: The Best Buy in Education; and Education Direction: How to Make the Right Decision.

Publish a list of recruiting questions and answers, and insert them in your church bulletin several times during the school year. For example:

1. How do Students Rank Academically? Students at Victory, over the past nine years, have scored on an average, no less than one and one half years above national norms.

Since the first graduating class, high school SAT and ACT test scores have averaged above the national norm with most students qualifying for academic scholarships.

Since 1987, Victory has graduated three National Merit Scholars, four semi-finalists, and three commended students. The average G.P.A. is 3.1 on a scale of 4.0.

2. Is the School Accredited? Victory holds recognition by two accrediting agencies. First, Victory has been accredited since 1983 by the International Christian Accrediting Association. Secondly, in 1989, Victory received accreditation with the State of Oklahoma Department of Education.

Parents provide the final test of accreditation. If a school is doing a good job, it will continue to grow. Over past five years, Victory has averaged over 700 students in grades K - 12th.

3. Do the Students have Bible Classes? All elementary students have Bible daily. The curriculum is from Radiant Press which includes Bible memory work. Chapels are presented weekly. At the secondary level, students attend Bible class three days per week; one day is spent in Chapel and one day in Bible seminar.

All 9th and 10th grade students must take a course in New and Old Testament survey. Upper-level Bible classes are geared to the needs of the student. Courses have included Christian Financial Concepts, Strategic Planning for Your Life, Practical Christian Living, Prayer, Missions, Evangelism, Names of God, Gifts of The Spirit, Fruits of The Spirit, etc.

A special music ministry class is available for those who have a special gift for music. Also, a missions class may be selected by those students interested in ministry and missions. Students have an opportunity to participate in ministry outreaches to the community, state and the nations. In the past, students have gone to: Costa Rica, Mexico, Jamaica, Guatemala, Belize, England and Germany.

Students have participated in street ministry, preaching, music, youth group training, physical labor, drama and counseling.

4. Are all Teachers Certified? All teachers must hold a degree in their area of expertise, as well as an Oklahoma teaching certificate for the subjects they teach.

In addition, Victory Christian School believes the type of training and range of experience, coupled with the lifestyle of the teacher, are important predictors of teaching success. It is our goal to have the best teachers possible. Presently, Victory Christian School teaching staff has an average of 12 years of experience. See Appendix C for additional Questions and Answers.

Special Bulletin

Feature your administrative and teaching staff in a special biographical sketch. Include such items as: names of members of the family, degrees earned, years of experience, special recognition, subjects or grade assigned (sometimes it is not possible to identify these until later in the summer), hobbies, favorite Scripture, etc.

Public Announcement

Acknowledge school staff as part of the Sunday service, giving their name, grade/subject to be taught, and when appropriate, a brief one- to two-minute testimony of what teaching in a Christian school means to them. Title this Sunday, Back-to-School day.

Have teaching staff available after the service at the school information table to answer questions prospective parents and students might have.

Ministry Mailings

Obtain permission to enclose a Christian education promotional item in the monthly ministry newsletter, Pastoral letter, or other ministry mailings. Consider enclosing promotional materials when paying vendors. Even if they have no interest in the school, they may know of someone who is interested.

Special Letters

Identify members of the church body who have children of school age; send a special letter introducing these families to the Christian school.

Don't overlook those people who may not be on the membership list, but have received services from the sponsoring church(es) - those who have attended seminars, church growth conferences, participated in children's and youth camps, been on the hospital visitation list, or those who have used the church building for funerals and weddings.

Telephone Calls

Make a telephone follow-up contact no less than three weeks following receipt of the introductory letter, answering questions and forwarding information on the school. The most effective time to call is on Saturdays between 9:00 a.m to 12:00 noon.

Publish the names of grade level unit leaders and teachers for parents to call for answers to questions about the school. Parents feel more freedom in talking to teachers rather than to administrators.

Preprinted Materials

You may write these articles yourself or obtain preprinted materials from the authors, 5747 South Utica, Tulsa, OK 74105 (918) 749-2157, or from Christian Schools Today, P.O. Box 264, Newtown Square, PA 19073 (215) 356-1910. Make sure you enclose a tear-off response section on all material.

Reading Materials

Purchase and give out to your parents to read and circulate books and materials on Christian schools: "What This Country Needs" and "Your Questions Answered About Christian Schools" by Paul A. Kienel are two popular promotional books.

When Abundant Life Christian School began, 50 copies were purchased and circulated among prospective parents. Of the 43 initial enrollments, 8 were a direct result of reading this book.

At Victory Christian School, we provide copies of these books to all our teaching staff, pastoral staff and care group leaders; we encourage them to share the books with prospective families. Enrolling one student is worth the time, effort and cost.

Information Table

Establish an information table in the church lobby. Display samples of curriculum, along with general information packets. Keep a contact card on each person who is given an information packet. Followup in no less than one week with a personal phone call. Have a member of the administrative team or faculty at the table before and after church services.

Be creative with the table. Assign this task to various departments of the school; e.g., elementary, Science, Math, English, etc. One of the best information table assignments at Victory was conducted by the Science teachers. Very few things attract as much attention as a working Van De Graff generator, biology specimens, or a full length human skeleton. A microscope with a slide and sign asking, "Can you identify the item on the slide?" will draw parent and student attention.

Christian School Day

Organize a Christian School Emphasis Day, and invite a special speaker who can effectively communicate the need for a quality Christian education; display samples of the curriculum and arrange tours of the facilities.

Christian Education Week

Christian Education Week began in 1930 when the International Council of Religious Education, representing 40 denominations and 30 state councils, chose the last week in

September as Christian Education Week. Its purpose was to focus attention on the importance of the teaching ministry of the church, in the church school and in the home. Consider the following:

1 Use this opportunity to focus attention on your Christian school.
2 Honor the work of the church educators.
3 Draw attention to faithful service, training and inspiration.
4 Plan a dedication or recognition service of worship in honor of all those who serve in Christian education.

Charter Class

A Charter Class Concept works well for a beginning school. Each new grade is advertised as a Charter Class. Consider placing the names of each charter class on a plaque. A specially designed parchment class roll can be given to each enrollee. The charter class concept becomes a tremendous acknowledgement during graduation, especially when students were in the first charter class and now are graduating.

Intercessory Prayer

Establish an intercessory prayer group for the school. The Word says, "...**The effectual fervent prayer of a righteous man availeth much**" (James 5:16).

A wide variety of organized formats for prayer are available - all school, before school, after school, noon hour, grade level, special interest (booster club, PTF, elementary), 24-hour prayer chain, student government, etc. Publish a list of the needs. Believe God for full enrollment at each grade level.

Plan Special Events

Provide special workshops on topics, such as "How to deal with Teenage Rebellion," "Skills for Single Parenting," "Avoiding the Homework Hassle," "Dealing with Peer Pressure," and "Effective Child Discipline."

These programs can be produced for very little cost by using school facilities and staff.

Other special recruiting events include:

1 A fashion show using students.

2 School sponsored valentine banquet.
3 Mother-daughter tea.
4 Father and son breakfast.
5 Craft fair.
6 Bike rallies.

Over-Printing of Yearbook Pages

Design your yearbook using a layout so you can over-print the first few pages. Use these as promotional materials. This is especially cost effective when using four-part color. Victory Christian School was able to over-print eight pages of four-part color at a cost of 16 cents per copy for 2,000 copies. The same four-part color layout published as a traditional pamphlet would have cost 75 cents per copy.

Enlist Grandparents

Sponsor a grandparents' day. This encourages grandparents to enroll their grandchildren. Produce a special brochure explaining how grandparents can sponsor their grandchildren, and offer a tuition discount to grandparents for first-time enrollments. Ask permission from the pastors of sponsoring churches to conduct a simple grandparent phone survey for everyone 55 years or older (See Figure 14).

Church Staff

It is much easier to promote the benefits of a Christian education when all full- and part-time staff children are enrolled in the school.

Clearly state the policy as part of your employment process. Established schools desiring to implement a similar policy should communicate the policy change no less than one year in advance of the date of implementation. This provides sufficient time for those who may not be in agreement with the policy to seek other employment. It also provides time for employees to adjust their budgets to accommodate the additional expense. Providing a 50 to 100 percent tuition reduction will lessen the financial impact of this policy on individual households, especially those with more than one child.

Hello. My name is ________________. I'm calling on behalf of Pastor __________ of ______________ (Church Name). We're doing a very short survey of grandparents. I'd like to get your response to five questions.

1. Do you have any grandchildren or great grandchildren?

2. Have any attended a Christian school?

3. Do you have any grandchildren or great grandchildren school age?

How many are attending public school? _____
How many are attending a Christian school? _____

4. What do you think is the greatest educational need facing your grandchildren?

5. Have you heard of (Name of Christian school) Grandparent sponsorship program?

If yes, or no, tell them: We would like to send you a brochure explaining this special opportunity. Let me confirm your address.

Confirm address:

Thank you for your time. God Bless You.

FIGURE 14 - Grandparent Phone Survey

Consider Home Schoolers

It is estimated there are more than 300,000 home schooled children in America (Wade, 1991). Every year, Christian schools have parents opting to home school their children. The loss of these students is one of the main reasons there is a reluctance on the part of some Christian schools to embrace the home school movement. On the other hand, every year Christian schools enroll home-schooled students.

Provide a Support Program

At some point in time, 95 percent of those parents who start home schooling will eventually place their children in a day school. Knowing this, it is advantageous for the Christian school to establish contact with these families. This contact will link parents and students to your school and enhance the likelihood of enrolling.

We realize the Christian school community is divided on how much support should be given, if any; eventually, every Christian school will have to take a position on the amount of support afforded to home schoolers. Those schools closely associated with a ministry that is underwriting the cost of the day school, directly or indirectly, fully or in part, have a special challenge - there will be those home schooling parents who are contributors to the ministry wanting to take advantage of the programs, facilities and resources the ministry provides. Furthermore, if the ministry is committed to meeting the needs of the body of believers, then some action towards families with home schoolers will be required.

Conduct Special Workshops

Schools can build relationships with home schoolers by providing parent workshops featuring school staff. Include topics such as: How to Select Curriculum, Keeping of Grade Books and other School Records, How to Find and Utilize Community and School Resources, How to Double Your Children's Grades, Dealing with Teenage Rebellion, Discipline in the Home School Setting, Effective Use of Instructional Aids and Working With Gifted Children.

Make Available School Facilities and Equipment

Other than the task of coordination, very little additional time or cost is necessary to make Christian school facilities and equipment available to home schoolers. Even if these facilities and equipment are not available during the school day, they can be made available after school and on weekends; athletic courts and fields, computer labs, science equipment and library resources are but a few items for consideration.

Someone once said, "What goes around comes around." Assisting home schoolers in meeting the education needs of their children will foster a closer relationship with the home schooling community. Eventually, some of these students will enroll in your school.

For more information on home schooling, see *The Home School Manual* by Theodore E. Wade (1991).

Use Your Alumni

For years, colleges have been effectively using alumni to recruit students. Most Christian schools ignore this concept mainly because of the extra effort it takes to establish a quality alumni program. Other schools avoid using alumni out of a concern alumni will "turn off" students.

What type of alumni would be the most successful in talking with prospective students? Select those who have a strong loyalty to the school and feel the school provided them with an educational experience they could not obtain in public school.

Selected and well-trained alumni can provide invaluable influence in recruiting new students. An alumni who persuades one student to attend is, in effect, assisting in raising $1,500 or more in contributions to the school, depending upon your tuition.

The following suggestions are provided to promote alumni participation in recruiting:

1 Encourage alumni to promote the school to school age children, friends and relatives.

2 Encourage children of alumni to attend - passing on the school tradition.

3 Recruit alumni for volunteers, coaching and tutoring. Invite them to special events, such as sporting events, award assemblies and graduation. Recognize alumni at these events.

4 Have alumni share a brief testimonial in church services or during intermissions at drama and music productions, at halftime during sporting events, or in chapels.

5 Use alumni to make phone calls.

6 Establish an alumni bulletin board featuring the alumni of the month. Provide pictures and a personal update. This will increase the awareness level of alumni support of the school. Sponsor an alumni day.

7 Place alumni on the school mailing list.

8 Dedicate an issue of the school newsletter or newspaper to alumni. Keeping them up to date and aware of new programs and changes is vital.

Keep up-to-date records on your alumni by conducting an annual alumni census. See Appendix D for a sample of an alumni census.

Contact Community Institutions and Organizations

In each community, there are dozens of service institutions and agencies which will be receptive to hearing about your school. Some of the more receptive are day care and preschool centers, community service agencies, and trade and professional associations.

Day Cares and Preschools

Check with your Chamber of Commerce for a listing of day cares and preschools in your city. If a special directory does not exist for day cares and preschools in your area, consider doing one as an annual fund-raiser, earning money through advertising in the directory.

1 Letters of Invitation. Send a special invitational letter and information packet to community day cares and preschool centers (See Figure 15).

2 Develop Regional Centers. If it is not possible to establish a day care center yourself, identify existing centers who would be open to a working relationship with your day school. The school (and ministry) would make referrals to these centers in exchange for the opportunity to have your school literature presented to parents whose children will be starting kindergarten (if the center does not offer a program for this age) or to those going into first grade. Conducting a "Getting Ready for First Grade" seminar is a creative way to benefit day care parents and at the same time present your school as one alternative.

Providing resources in the way of special speakers, library loan programs and joint purchase of supplies, will help build a strong relationship with day cares and preschools.

Community Service Agencies

The "Welcome Wagon," Chamber of Commerce and other organizations have contact with families moving to the

(Letterhead)

(Date)

(Inside Address)

Dear (Name of Director):

As we approach the end of the school year, many of your children will be attending elementary school in the fall. We would like the opportunity to present Victory Christian School to your parents. Many of them are looking for an alternative to public school.

Enclosed is a sample of an information we would like to make available to your parents. You will also find a list of free workshops we would be more than happy to conduct for your parents and those students going to elementary school. We have found a very positive response from parents who have attended our workshops. As you know, the transition from preschool to elementary can be very difficult. Together we can make a difference!

I will be calling in a couple days to schedule a meeting.

Meanwhile, if you have any questions, please call.

Sincerely,

Superintendent

FIGURE 15 - Day Care Invitation

community. Provide these agencies with copies of parent information packets.

List the name of your school in directories published by these agencies, such as a directory of private schools.

Trade and Professional Associations

Industrial trade groups, professional associations, technical societies and credit unions offer community information services and newsletters to their members. Ask to be included in community awareness materials; e.g., directories, member packets, placement services, etc.

Obtain permission to set up a display table at a local convention. The likelihood of actually enrolling from a school booth at a convention or trade school is very slim. However, give all those who come to your booth a take-away item with your school name on it. This places your name before the community.

Go After Future Students

There is another group of students many Christian schools overlook - students between the ages of birth to four years of age. Response mail services have ways of identifying this group of potential students. Developing strategies to introduce the Christian school to this population of students will pay handsome rewards in the future.

Consider such strategies as: sending a specially-designed card or making phone calls to parents of newborns, sponsoring a preschool preparation night, parenting workshops, preschool olympics, health and safety awareness seminars and preschool book fair.

Your school can sponsor a school home-based enrichment program to be used in the home with children ages three to six; a program titled "WINGS" helps children develop skills that have remained undeveloped, builds self-esteem and confidence, enhances the quality of family life and helps children reach their full potential by preparing them for success in school. Offering this program through the school establishes a supportive relationship with the home and will enhance the opportunity of these children enrolling in your school. For more information on the WINGS program, contact the authors.

Conduct an Open House

Broadly defined, an open house is a school-sponsored gathering open to the public. A well-orchestrated open house is the most cost-effective means of recruiting students. It has the potential for recruiting the greatest number of students in a single event, since those who come to an open house already have a genuine interest in Christian education.

Holding the open house in the school provides a distinct advantage; you can include tours, demonstrations and special presentations.

Schools just starting need to provide as many open houses as possible. Established schools should plan for no less than four open houses. The first open house should take place the first week in March. This is important since many Christian schools are beginning to announce re-enrollment for the coming year. It is difficult to get a parent to your open house if they have already enrolled at another school and paid an enrollment fee. When parents make a financial commitment to attend a school, they usually attend.

Conduct the second open house the first week in May. This provides the last opportunity for parents to view the school before it prepares to close for the summer. Many parents will still be undecided about enrolling in a Christian school and will have many questions to be answered.

The first week in August is a good opportunity for an open house. There will still be a large number of families who have not decided about re-enrollment or enrolling for the very first time. Many new families will be moving into the city. Since classes will not be in session, it is important to have several classrooms set up for the first day of school. Ask returning teachers who are available to participate in the open house.

Hold another open house just before the end of the semester. This provides a natural break in the academic year for those parents who are considering mid-term placement.

Open House Tips

The following strategies are important for successful open houses.

1. **Exposure**. The size of the turnout for an open house is difficult to predict. The secret to a bulging attendance is exposure, exposure and more exposure. Use newspaper ads, TV spots, neighborhood door hangers and other advertising methods to publicize the event.

Be creative in your efforts. Try using an 18 foot advertising balloon; invite a local radio station to broadcast from the open house. Church-sponsored schools will find a personal invitation from the pastor to be very effective.

2. **Building.** First impressions are lasting. Clean and neat classrooms, restrooms and hallways are important.

Don't overlook the outside. Get in your car and drive up to the school building and view it through the eyes of parents and students as if it were the very first time they saw it. What do you see? Is the parking lot clean? Are the school grounds free of paper and items that look out of place? Are the windows clean? It is amazing what clean windows will do for a building. Would some fresh paint make a difference? How about some flowers next to the entrance?

3. **Involvement.** Involve as many people as possible - administrators, teachers and parents. Make sure they are all well-dressed and well-groomed.

Use elementary and high school students as greeters, ushers, hallway monitors, etc. Friendly, caring, polite students send a strong message to those who are visiting. Direct communication with students in a discussion group following the main program is a good technique for attracting upper-level students who otherwise may not have been interested in changing schools despite the enthusiastic efforts of parents.

Students representing the school must have all the pertinent information they need and must know the message to be communicated.

4. **Variety.** Remember, the lecture approach results in no more than 15 percent retention; therefore, use a lot of visuals, charts, pictures, slides, and demonstrations by various groups of students. Display as much student work as is possible - bulletin boards, hallways and ceiling.

5. **Gifts for the children**. Very few items win the hearts of young and old as a helium-filled balloon. Everyone who comes through the door should receive a balloon with the school name. You can add other messages on the balloon as you so desire - "See you in the Fall!" "To our very special guests." Use the school logo and motto.

You might say, "Yes, but all of this costs money." Consider the answer to this question, "Do you think the financial commitment you make to your open house would result in one student attending?" A hundred dollars worth of balloons is a small price to pay when it results in at least one student enrolling. Furthermore, business research shows when gifts are used in promotions, people are more inclined to give a favorable response. In addition to balloons, try book markers, pins, banners, pencils, hats, etc.

Some might think, "We don't believe in using bribes." Bribes are things you earn for devious behavior. A better word is rewards. The message given is, "We appreciate you coming, and come back and see us again."

6. Demonstrations. Nothing catches the eyes of prospective students better than a demonstration from another group of students. This might be a special greeting from the cheerleaders, or a presentation by a phonics drill team; keep the demonstration to no more than two- to three-minutes.

7. Personal Testimony. Many new families enroll because of the personal testimony of an enthusiastic parent or student. Find someone whose Christian school testimony relates to those who will be visiting. Testimonies might focus in part on God's financial provision, positive changes in academics and behavior, positive changes in the family or the spiritual life of students and parents.

Don't overlook a personal word from graduates attending college who are recipients of special awards from the school. Send out a special invitation requesting their participation. Confirm this well in advance of the open house. Having a graduate who is now married and sending his own children to the school will have a lasting influence upon a decision for enrollment.

8. Information packets. When putting together information packets, ask yourself this question, "What will be the very first impression visitors get from this packet?"

Communicating a central message in a concise, neat fashion is very important. Develop the literature contained in the packet to meet the needs of parents and students who are the target for the literature.

Be careful of "overload." Some schools try to put everything but the science lab sink in the visitor's packet. Our experience has shown the most important component of the information packet is basic school information (size, history, philosophy and programs offered).

Use an attractive folder containing a simple welcome letter from the superintendent or pastor, followed by a copy of the program, school brochure, fact sheet and attendance. We do not recommend including an enrollment form or a cost sheet in the packet. We have found it becomes a distraction to parents.

When parents see the cost before they see the program, the immediate reaction is, "We cannot afford this!" This kind of response influences their perspective of everything else happening during the open house. Providing a copy of the tuition and fee schedules at the end of the open house leaves parents with the perception, "It is worth the cost."

When you place in the Open House folder everything the parents need to know about the school, they will ask very few questions. We have found withholding key pieces of information invites parents to ask questions. In so doing, they get a personal response and an opportunity to get to know teachers and administrators. Many times, it is the personal touch from teachers, administrators, parents and helping students which convinces parents to enroll.

Since you will always have parents who are very reserved in asking questions, place in the hands of parents (on the way out), a sheet containing answers to questions most frequently asked by parents (See Appendix C). This will also give parents a valuable piece of communication to take home - something the Holy Spirit can easily call back to their remembrance.

Make enrollment packets available at the door when parents leave. Withholding this important packet until the parents exit provides an opportunity for you to collect an attendance card to be used for followup. Visitors simply turn in a completed card in exchange for an enrollment packet including applications, tuition and fee schedule.

9. Goodies. No open house is complete without a time of informal fellowship around a tray of cookies, punch and coffee. Put your best "people persons" where the goodies are - people who are full of the life of God and show the most enthusiasm for the school.

Make sure they are well informed about the school. A preparation meeting prior to the open house is highly recommended. We also recommend assigning administrators to this area to greet the visitors individually and answer any questions they may have.

10. Be Realistic. It is easy for a school to oversell itself. Since most parents realize no school is perfect, present parents and students all pertinent information without distortion.

Simply let parents know up front there will be room for improvement, and the school is committed to making the school the very best it can be for their children.

Why is it important to be realistic? The long-term goal extends far beyond recruitment. To be successful, a school must not only attract students, but it must retain them. A realistic approach will result in more satisfied parents and students.

11. Atmosphere. Above all else, provide a relaxed, comfortable atmosphere for all participants. The image you want to project is "the school is doing well and is blessed to be given the responsibility of providing a quality Christian education for their children."

Advertising for an Open House

It continues to amaze us; given all the advertising Victory Christian School does, one still finds Christians who have been in Tulsa for several years and have never heard about the school.

When asked how much should be spent on advertising, our answer has been, "as much as possible." The net effect of students enrolling usually is enough to offset most advertising costs.

Apply the principle contained in the sower (Matthew 13:1-23) to mass media advertising. Although the farmer sows seed in four different places, only one of the places accomplishes its purpose. In the remaining three places, the seed produces no results. However, the seed which fell on the good ground produced fruit thirty-, sixty-, and one-hundred fold. Was it worth the time, effort and expense to sow the seed? Plant your seed; then believe God for the one-hundred fold return.

Employ an Informed, Positive Secretary and Receptionist

A.A. Baker (1979) offers the following advice:

> "You may create much interest in your school through promotions, advertising, brochures, and fliers. All, however, will come to naught if you do not have someone in your office to turn interest into the positive action of enrolling the students. A bright, positive secretary with a pleasant telephone voice and the right answers is a must.

It is this person who is the key to follow-up contacts of enrollment in your Christian school. You need to be certain that the person who answers the telephone in your office is helpful, friendly, has right answers and can satisfy the people who are calling concerning your school. She should take the initiative to give all the advantages of your school as well as answering questions" (p. 143).

Be Ready to Answer Questions

What questions will parents ask? Prepare front-line school staff with answers to the following questions:

1. ***In what ways does the school combine Christianity and learning?*** Answers should go beyond a modest "required chapel," to present a sophisticated program of seeking God's truth in all subjects.

2. ***What are the discipline procedures?*** Parents need to know the school uses a wide variety of methods of discipline with the goal being self-discipline.

3. ***What is the average number of years the faculty has been teaching?*** Stress the wide variety of experience, not a beginning staff just out of college. Compute the average years of experience, and have it available as part of the fact sheet.

4. ***How many present faculty have been here on staff five or more years?*** High turnover of staff indicates a potential red flag to parents. Turnover rates above 30 percent will need to be explained.

5. ***Are the teachers required to accept the authority of Scripture, or are they merely "Christian" in a general civilized sense?*** State the spiritual employment standards of the school.

6. ***What minority groups are enrolled in school?*** Know the percent and the anticipated percent. Remember your non-discriminatory statement.

7. ***Must all children come from Christian homes, or are some non-Christian homes represented?*** This depends on your admissions standards. Although your school may only accept students from Christian homes, it is well to point out you have received applications from others. This indicates a respect for the academic standards of the school.

8. *What rules will my child be expected to follow? Is there a dress code or a student handbook we could look over?* Parents will take your response and compare it to what is expected in the home and how their individual child will respond. Prepare to deal with a wide variation between home and school expectations.

9. *What percentage of last year's students are returning this year?* Know the exact figure. If there has been a high turnover, know the reason.

10. *To what colleges have recent high school graduates gone?* Parents will be looking for colleges they respect. Provide a listing of colleges as part of your fact sheet.

11. *How do test scores in basic academic areas compare with other schools in the community?* Know where your school stands in comparison to local, state and national standards. Also, know the reasons private schools score higher - environment, strong discipline, influence of the home, strong supportive working relationship between home and school, etc.

12. *Are there any programs for advanced placement of exceptional students?* Include a listing of honors, accelerated and advanced placement programs in your fact sheet.

13. *How many different subjects would a teacher in upper grades usually teach?* A teacher trained at the secondary level with a major in science and a minor in math can probably teach four or five courses in those fields, but to assign him to teach in four content areas such as science, math, Bible, and history where four to six different preparations are required will reduce the overall effectiveness of the teacher.

14. *What are some of the extracurricular activities?* Include this listing in your student handbook.

15. *Who controls the school?* If it is a board, know who are on the board and make a list available to parents. Know when the board meets. Know which board members have children in your school.

16. *Have there been problems with drugs?* There is always the possibility some student may bring drugs to school. Saying there are "No" drugs, especially for a large school, tells parents the school doesn't really know. Rather, point out your school's position on drugs as specified in your student handbook.

17. ***Is there a denominational or sectarian emphasis in the religious teaching?*** State your curriculum and religious position. A clear statement of faith should be available in your student handbook. Stress interdenominational rather than non-denominational.

18. ***Is the school a part of a state or national association of schools?*** Know your school's position on this issue.

19. ***Is the school accredited or registered with the state education department?*** We encourage all schools to seek accreditation, especially from a Christian Accreditation organization, such as the International Christian Accrediting Association, or Association of Christian Schools International. For a complete discussion of accreditation and teacher certification, see *Legal Requirements for Christian Schools* by the authors.

20. ***How often are the textbooks updated?*** Most paperback books are good for one to two years, hard bound- five years. Share with parents your textbook review procedures.

21. ***How much involvement are the parents expected to take in the life of the school?*** Stress the importance of parents being involved in the educational experience of their children, whether it is at school or in the home. Then, if school involvement is required, explain the nature of the commitment.

22. ***Are the teachers certified by the state or working toward it?*** Stress the importance of academic and professional preparation as well as experience of your staff. Make available to your parents a staff roster with these facts.

23. ***What contacts are maintained with non-Christian schools, such as athletic competition or debating meets?*** Parents may be concerned about the negative effects of non-Christian students. Focus your comments on the idea of your students being very strong witnesses in a hurting and Christless world and the importance of witnessing through student activities and athletic events.

24. ***Can the school supply the names of some parents in my neighborhood with whom I could discuss the school?*** Contact parents ahead of time, and request permission to include their names on a "parent reference" list to be given out to prospective

parents. Select those parents who have been supportive of the school and have served in leadership positions.

25. ***What led to the founding of the school?*** State the vision of the school; provide written copies of the vision. Consider producing an audio tape explaining the vision, one that can be given and listened to by parents and students being enrolled.

26. ***What standards does the school have for acceptance?*** Be careful not to give the impression that your school is an "elitist" or "problem student" school.

27. ***How closely have operations come to breaking even financially in the last two years?*** Since most parents do not understand audit or budget reports, have available pie charts and graphs highlighting summary data.

28. ***What experience and academic credentials does the headmaster or principal have?*** Leadership is very important to most parents. Administrative staff should hold a master's degree or be working towards one. If administrative staff have less than three years of experience as administrators, point out how other experiences have and will benefit the school; e.g., management positions, self-employed, teaching experience, etc. Include experience summary data as part of your general staff information sheet. Encourage your staff to consider using the Oral Roberts University Summer Institute to obtain their master's degree. Write for more information on this special summer program.

29. ***What role does the pastor of the church play in the school?*** Leadership of the pastor is very important for most parents. Explain some of the activities of the pastor as they relate to the school; e.g., sharing in chapel, teaching, counseling, etc.

30. ***What is the teacher-student ratio?*** Although some schools offer small classes as proof of "quality" education, research has yet to substantiate the fact that a given class size is a guarantee of educational success of all children. The challenge with pupil-teacher ratio is it fails to take into account staff, other than teachers, who have a significant impact upon the lives of your students - for example, the administrator, guidance counselor, or chaplain. The answer is to use a staff-student ratio. This would take into account all professional staff who are influencing the lives of the students.

Create a Special Visitors Area

Set up a special area for prospective parents and students as they visit the school.

1 This may be an unused classroom, corner of the library, small alcove, or reception area in the main hallway.

2 Make use of available recruitment literature and audio-visual programs.

3 Display school trophies, special awards, sport uniforms, yearbooks and plenty of pictures.

4 Students, parents, alumni and other volunteers can manage the center.

Keep Good Records

The key to effective followup is a systematic tracking system. This system should include a tracking card (3x5) on all individuals requesting information about the school.

1 Collect their name, address, zip, date of contact, phone number, children's names and grades.

2 Classify each family in one of three categories: plan to attend, not attending, or undecided.

3 For the "undecided group," further categorize these according to the reason; e.g. financial, transportation, relocation out of the community or miscellaneous.

These groups become the priority target groups for additional followup. Transfer all of this data into a master tracking log.

Effective recruiting involves going after every possible student. Don't prejudge any family by saying, "They will not be interested in sending their children to our school."

Improve Customer Relations

5

The main recruiting effort of established schools comes through more than one giant campaign during registration. Rather, it is happening every day of the school year. Each day, there are 20 to 30 little newspapers going home from each classroom; they are the walking, talking, real live recruiters of your school - the students. What kind of headlines do your students take home to parents and community? Are they:

- **Teacher Blows His Cool: Three Students Injured.**
- **Lack of Understanding Breeds Bitterness, Nobody Listens.**
- **Fairness - A Forgotten Trait.**
- **Teacher Builds Student Self-Esteem.**
- **A School With A Heart.**
- **Caring Teachers Receive Rich Dividends.**
- **Love, Acceptance And Forgiveness - A Way of Life.**

The day-to-day happenings in school influence what students share with their parents and friends, the results of which can have a negative or positive influence on perceptions of the school.

The stronger the relationship among students, staff and parents, the better a school's chances are of recruiting and retaining students. Relationships can be improved by fostering customer satisfaction, meeting the placement needs of parents and resolving challenges when they arise.

Foster Customer Satisfaction

Regardless of the size of your school or number of years it has been in existence, no recruiting or retaining strategy compares to the influence of a satisfied school family. The world of business would call these people satisfied customers. They are the ones who keep returning; they like the service, the quality product and the price. They are the ones who tell others where the best buys are found.

Consider your own situation. Whether you are looking for a good dentist, doctor, or an auto mechanic, you ask around. Now, consider the Christian community. If they were to look for a quality Christian School, they would ask Christians whose children are already attending a Christian school. If they have been a satisfied customer, they would recommend your school.

Producing more satisfied customers results from making good decisions based on what is best for students, valuing input from parent and student opinion, establishing a caring school climate, meeting the placement needs of parents and effectively resolving challenges when they arise.

Base Decisions on Student Needs

So often, decisions schools make are based on convenience for school staff, ease of curriculum management, or efficiency of operations, rather than on what is in the best interest of students and parents. For example, requiring high school students to sit with their own grade level in the cafeteria is a decision made to facilitate better teacher supervision. Making these types of decisions and policies sends a negative message home: "They don't listen," "They don't care," "They don't understand," or "Why did they do that?"

Sometimes a decision may be made without giving parents or students the necessary background leading to the decision or new policy; as a result, they may form a biased perception. Perceptions parents and students have of a particular situation are very real and capable of influencing others. Negative perceptions lead to negative reports affecting future enrollment.

Most negative reports are a result of second-hand information or wrong information about the school, staff, or programs. The way your school responds to negative reports is very important.

The following suggestions are offered:

1 **Be calm**. Do not become defensive, justify the school's position, cut the parent or student off, or classify him as a maverick.
2 **Hear the complaint**. Listen with interest and understanding, and either correct the issue or explain the school's position.
3 **Study parent and student complaints**. Quality time invested in parent and student complaints can pay handsome rewards.
4 **Ask for parent and student help**. Some of your greatest supporters will be those students and parents who get involved in solving challenge situations.
5 **Value their opinion**. Treat parents as stockholders of the school organization; after all, without them, there would most likely not be a school.

Identify Problems

What can a school do to identify challenge areas, and how can you make the necessary corrections before they can become negative influences on student retention?

At times, those who are able to make changes are the last ones to find out about challenges. For example, a school administrator can walk down the hallways, observe classrooms, chat with students and visit with parents; it would appear, from all outward evidence, everything seems "just fine." Only a small percent of the parents or students are willing to confront administrators first hand with what is "really happening" in the school. Consider the following resolves.

Paper and Pencil Surveys, Questionnaires, Rating Forms

These are very easy to construct. Develop a survey like the one found in Appendix E. Send it home to all families before the end of the first semester. The survey results will help identify critical areas needing improvement. Make the necessary adjustments before the start of the second semester. Survey results provide information to help close the "back door" to mid-term and end-of-year transfers. Publishing the results of the survey in the school newspaper or newsletter gives all who participate a positive feeling about the value of their input.

The following guidelines will enhance the effective use of a mail survey.

1 **Identify the specific challenges.** Decide if the survey is the best tool to collect the kind of information that will lead to a solution.

2 **State in writing the goals of the survey.**

3 **Decide which groups you want to survey.**

4 **Determine the size of your sample.** Keep in mind at least a 50 percent response rate is necessary to have confidence in the results. If it is not possible to survey an entire group, i.e., all junior high students, use a random sample.

5 **Construct your survey.** Be brief, specific, pay attention to clarity and use structured rather than open-ended questions whenever possible.

6 **Pretest your survey.** Have teachers, parents and students complete a sample form and offer suggestions.

7 **Mail survey.** The more you spend for postage, the greater response you will receive; first class brings greater results than using a school permit number or third class. Include a stamped, self-addressed envelope and a letter explaining the importance of participation.

8 **Mail reminder post cards.** Do this three or four days after survey. Do a second mailing to non-responders two to three weeks after the first mailing.

9 **Tabulate and analyze the returns.** Count responses, calculate percentages, and write summary statements.

10 **Arrange the concerns in order of occurrence.**

11 **Identify priority topics for change or improvement.**

12 **Develop strategies for change.**

13 **Carry out the strategies.**

14 **Evaluate the results.**

Victory conducted a comprehensive mail survey of all parents. The results of the survey were very revealing. Converting the results to a list of priorities and adding these to a five-year plan for improvement was very beneficial. The cover letter for this survey is found in Figure 16.

This comprehensive mail survey consists of 69 questions, providing over 120 different pieces of information. All of the

LETTERHEAD

Dear VCS Parent:

Will you do us a favor?

We are conducting a survey among the parents of Victory Christian School students. The survey is being conducted for the Administrative Council and Parent Advisory Board of VCS.

The purpose of the research is to learn how well parents feel the goals of VCS are being met at this stage in VCS's development. It is the desire of VCS's Administrative Council and Parent Advisory Board to continue with what is perceived as good and strengthen the areas you feel could be improved. Therefore, your honest and straight-forward opinions will mean a great deal to the overall direction that VCS takes.

Your answers will be very important to the accuracy of the research. It will take only a short time to answer the simple questions on the enclosed questionnaire and return it in the envelope provided.

Of course, all answers are strictly confidential. You will notice the questionnaire you fill out does not have a place for your name on it. It does have a number. The number will be used to enable us to check off the names of parents who have completed the questionnaire. These numbers will provide us a way to follow up and remind parents whose "numbers" have not been returned, who may have overlooked filling out and sending in their survey. Never will a person's name be associated with an individual questionnaire, nor will the faculty, administration, or Parent Advisory Board have any access to the numbers or names.

We are asking for questionnaires to be filled out and put back in the mail to us within three days of your receiving it, if at all possible. The general findings will be communicated to the parents upon completion of the study.

Thank you very much for your help and cooperation.

Sincerely,

Superintendent

FIGURE 16 - Parent Survey Cover Letter

responses are tabulated and placed on a computer. Various statistical tests are performed on all responses, along with graphic presentations. A copy of the complete survey is available upon request from the authors who are also available to conduct the survey on behalf of any interested Christian schools and provide the school with detailed analysis.

When this survey was conducted at Victory Christian School, parents rated the physical education program as needing the most improvement. These results motivated the school to write a comprehensive physical education program called ZOE Health Fitness (Ward, 1983). This program is being used in nearly a hundred Christian Schools across America.

The Re-enrollment Survey

If students make it successfully through the first semester, chances are, they will remain in school for the entire year. It is during the third quarter that students and parents begin to formulate decisions about re-enrolling.

Most schools begin re-enrolling in March or April. For those families who experience conflict with the school, their attitude may be, "We'll give them one more quarter to see if things will improve. If they don't make any changes, we're not coming back." Unfortunately, many of those who have these attitudes fail to communicate them to those who have the authority to make changes. A simple re-enrollment survey administered to students and parents will help identify these attitudes and areas needing improvement (see Figure 17).

Telephone Surveys and Exit Interviews

There is nothing more enlightening than an exit interview. Many times parents withdraw their children out of frustration with a particular teacher, poor grades, misinterpreted policies, lack of understanding and a whole host of other reasons. A few quality minutes given to parents who are withdrawing their children could prevent a withdrawal.

During the beginning of the second week in school, I was walking out of my office, and I noticed a father withdrawing his son. I asked if I could have a word with him. The father commented on how unhappy his son was with school. Everyday his son was coming home crying and wanted to return to public school. After a little questioning, I found out the reason Andy was so unhappy - he was unable to make it to his classes on time; he kept forgetting his locker combination, and was forever getting

Reenrollment Survey

Grade level you are presently in:________ Date __________

Please respond to the following questions:

1. Select one of the following by placing a check mark after the letter:
At this point in time -

A. ____ I am planning on returning to Victory next year.
B. ____ I am undecided about returning to Victory next year.
C. ____ I am definitely not returning to Victory next year.

If you checked letter C, what is (are) the reason(s) you are definitely not returning to Victory next year? ________________

2 In your time at Victory as a student what do you feel are the school's strengths?________________

3. What do you feel contributes most to students wanting to leave Victory?________________

4. What do you feel the school could change, adjust, alter, or improve to make Victory a place where students want to come and stay through graduation?________________

5. What improvements do we need to make in the following areas:

A. Administration: ________________
B. Teachers: ________________
C. Athletics: ________________
D. Discipline Procedures ________________
E. Subjects and courses: ________________
F. Chapels: ________________
G. Rules: ________________
H. Spiritual Aspects: ________________
I. Other Areas ________________

FIGURE 17 - Re-Enrollment Survey

lost in the building. Andy had been in a self-contained classroom up through the sixth grade, and he had never passed between classes each period. Complicating matters was his short stature; he was overwhelmed by taller high school students and could hardly see his way down the crowded hallways. When Andy was given a little reassurance, a few pointers on remembering his combination, the best times to return to his locker and was teamed up with another 7th grader on the same schedule, he was a new boy. When you talk to Andy today, you will find the only way he's going to leave school is by graduating. One of the best policies a school can have is requiring all parents to participate in an exit

(School Logo)

Date ________________ Grade Level ________________

Student Name ________________________________

Date first enrolled ________________________________

Number of years and months at school ________________
Homeroom Teacher ________________________________

Reason for withdrawing: (Financial, transportation, moving, etc)

____

____

What needs to change in order to remain in school?

____

____

What was the most enjoyable aspect of the school?

____

____

Transition follow-up date ________________

FIGURE 18 - Exit Interview

interview with the administrator before withdrawing (See Figure 18). There may be an Andy in your school.

Rap Sessions with Administrative Staff

The primary rumor control officer is the administrator. Deal with second-hand information and wrong information during rap sessions with the students. In conducting a rap session:

1 Make it as informal as possible; consider one grade level at a time.

2 Take written, unsigned questions if it will help put everyone at ease.

3 Prepare to incorporate in the rap session clarification of issues previously brought to your attention.

Personal Questioning

While standing by the door during dismissal, the question was asked of a kindergarten parent, "Have you re-enrolled for next year?" The parent answered, "Well, not yet. We may not be returning next year." After probing for a reason, the parent revealed his displeasure with the behavior of his daughter and felt her behavior had regressed since coming to school. He attributed this to lack of discipline in the classroom. Before the school year was over, we were able to affect a positive change in the classroom, and as a result, the parent re-enrolled his daughter.

Insertion of Response Forms with Report Cards

A good time to gain input from parents concerning academics is during grading periods. Attaching a simple response form to each child's report card is a very simple process (see Figure 19); yet, it yields valuable information. Use this information in planning for the next grading period. Have parents return the response forms to teachers, the office, or place them in the mail.

Suggestion Box

Place a suggestion box where students and parents can provide new ideas for the improvement of the school.

Study Groups

Organize staff and parent meetings around the study of challenges and the improvement of the school program.

Depend Upon the Quickening of the Holy Spirit

The Word says, The Lord "...**will bring to light the hidden things of darkness, and will make manifest the counsels of the hearts...**" (1 Corinthians 4:5). Expect God to reveal hidden things. In one of our schools, items and supplies began disappearing from lockers, teacher and student desks, the school office and science lab. This was upsetting to many students, teachers and parents. One family, whose child was missing a very expensive jacket, was considering withdrawing from school if something wasn't done about the missing items.

As much as the staff tried, we were unsuccessful at catching the thief. One day, some magnifying glasses were taken from the science lab. Questioning every single high school student as to the whereabouts of the missing items seemed appropriate. During the questioning, I asked the Holy Spirit to quicken my spirit to the person who was responsible for the missing items. The moment I began to question Danny, I had a knowing in my spirit "this student was the one responsible for all of the missing items."

The more I questioned him, the more he denied having anything to do with the missing items. About 30 minutes after school was out, I was setting at my desk doing some paper work when my spirit was quickened to go outside behind the school

LETTERHEAD

Dear Parents:

Upon completing our first grading period, we would like your input about how you feel about various aspects of our academic program. Your responses and suggestions are of value as we plan for our next quarter.

After completing this survey, please return it to school with your son or daughter. All responses are considered confidential.

Grade Level your child(ren) is/are in: ____________________

1. On an average, how many minutes per night does your child spend on homework?

Child 1 - Grade ___: ___________ minutes
Child 2 - Grade ___: ___________ minutes
Child 3 - Grade ___: ___________ minutes

2. Overall, the grades your child received were:

Child 1: As expected ___ Below ___ Above expectations ___
Child 2: As expected ___ Below ___ Above expectations ___
Child 3: As expected ___ Below ___ Above expectations ___

3. Which area of study did your child enjoy the most?

Child 1: ____
Child 2: ____
Child 3: ____

4. In which area of study did they have the greatest challenge?

Child 1: ____
Child 2:____
Child 3: ____

5. If you could change any aspect of the academic program for next quarter, what would you change and why?

____
____
____

6. What changes would you make in order for your child to be more successful in school?

____
____
____
____

FIGURE 19 - Report Card Survey

building to an area by the air-conditioning units. There I found Danny with the magnifying glasses in his hands. He was shocked to see me. When his eyes met mine, the first words that came out of my mouth were, "God is so concerned about you and what is happening in your life, the Holy Spirit led me right to your hiding place. You can never hide from God."

The easiest way to deal with Danny would have been to ask him to withdraw, "I'm sorry we don't want any thieves in our Christian school." In fact, there were several parents who were asking for this very consequence. After praying as to what to do with Danny, the Holy Spirit would not give me the release to remove Danny from the school.

Through the work of the Holy Spirit, the items missing from the school were recovered, and the hidden behaviors in Danny's life were exposed. And in so doing, Danny could receive the necessary counseling to help him become all God intended. Danny repented of his sin, harmony returned to the school and no children were withdrawn.

Having a commitment to meeting student needs doesn't mean a school has to compromise any standards; it doesn't mean students and parents run the school; it means their needs cannot be ignored. Through the work of the Holy Spirit, these needs can be identified and answers found.

Meet the Placement Needs of Parents

A second method for improving relationships among students, staff and parents is by meeting the placement needs of parents.

The reason most parents enroll (re-enroll) a child in a Christian school is not in obedience to the awesome command of the Lord to teach and train a child in the way he should go (Proverbs 22:6). Most parents who decide to place their children in a Christian school do so for other reasons. The three most often reported motivations for enrolling in a Christian school are academic, behavioral and spiritual.

How well is your school doing in meeting the placement needs of parents? A positive answer to the following placement concerns will increase the likelihood of recruiting and retaining quality students.

Academic

1 Are students perceived by administrators and teachers as being capable of making significant academic progress?

2 Does the staff agree that academics are a high priority?

3 Are there strong routines for keeping order and disruptions at a minimum? Is there an attitude which protects classes from interruptions?

4 Has a strong learning environment become a part of the tradition lending itself to a positive reputation?

5 Does the instruction provide for variety and enjoyment of learning?

6 Do teachers and programs meet the individual learning needs of the students?

7 Are the parents getting their money's worth?

8 Are teachers well prepared for class?

9 Do they start and end class promptly?

10 Is homework regularly assigned and checked?

11 Are teachers cooperative and supportive of others?

12 Is the tone of the staff businesslike and professional, yet interesting to students?

13 Is the pupil-teacher ratio within acceptable limits?

Behavioral

1 Are discipline policies established, communicated and enforced fairly and consistently?

2 Is there a clear set of rules and consequences for violation of these rules?

3 Is the importance of regular attendance, promptness and respect for teachers fostered?

4 Is there a high level of help, concern and friendship directed towards students?

5 Do teachers talk openly with students, trust them and express an interest in their lives?

6 Is Christ-like character being instilled in the lives of students?

7 Are students being trained to be self-disciplined?

Spiritual

1 Is prayer incorporated as an essential ingredient in each classroom?
2 Is the uncompromised Word of God integrated as the foundation for all of learning and behavior?
3 Is the Holy Spirit given right of way in the educational process?
4 Does the teacher maintain a lifestyle that is Christ-like and make a personal relationship with Christ a top priority?
5 Does the anointing of God reside in the classrooms?
6 Are the students taught how to apply the Word of God to their daily life?
7 Are students discipled?

Most Christian educators will agree, parents telling parents the good news about the school is the best student retention tool. Satisfied parents will speak out positively about the school regardless of what administrators and teachers say.

Solicit Parent Participation

Parents in Christian schools show a concern for their child's education and are willing to become involved, especially when involvement benefits their child(ren).

The only risk for the school when parents volunteer on a regular basis is the opportunity to see "what is happening in the kitchen." Anyone who has worked in a restaurant knows there is a difference between what happens out where the customers are and what goes on in the kitchen. Out where the customers are there is peace and tranquility. What happens in the kitchen, is another story. When parents get in the kitchen they will notice inconsistencies between what is being said and what is really happening in the school. When both what goes on in the kitchen (offices, teacher lounge) and what goes on in the serving area (classrooms) are in harmony, parents will notice and will be positive supporters of the school, its staff and programs.

Opportunities for Service

Historically, parent involvement has been restricted to room mothering, chaperoning field trips and Parent-Teacher-

Fellowships. Today's parents can still find usefulness in these areas; however, expanding the opportunities for service fosters a greater chance to win parent support.

Parents can function in almost any aspect of the school program. They can share their career, hobbies and artistic or technical expertise in the classroom. Leading workshops, sponsoring parent classes, listening to students read, serving as tutors, overseeing clubs and hobby days, running a copy service, making teaching aids, helping in the publication of the school newsletter, newspaper, or yearbook are but a few non-traditional areas of service.

Conduct a parent volunteer service survey (See Figure 20); find out what parents want to do, then put them to work. There are two actions a school should never do. They should never sign parents up to help and not call upon their services and assign a parent volunteer who sits all day with no task to do. These parents may be more harmful to school recruitment than having no parental involvement at all (Krajewski, et al., 1983).

Parent-Teacher Fellowship

Any school can have an active, strong Parent-Teacher Fellowship; all it requires is a little planning. In formulating a parent support group, consider the following:

1. **Identify the group's purpose and set goals**. Focus the group on improving the school and tackling problems.
2. **Provide a definite structure**. Publish an agenda; start and stop on time.
3. **Obtain enthusiastic leadership**. Appoint those parents who can keep members encouraged and inspired.
4. **Foster teamwork**. Teamwork between parents and teachers, home and school pays handsome dividends; parents are delighted when they know everyone is focusing on what is best for the students.
5. **Problem solve**. Accomplish this by helping parents form study groups to research problems and bring recommendations to the administration or board. Victory has a Parent Action Team that meets monthly. Two team members repre-

Parent Ministry Survey
(One Per Family)

Realizing that parents are a valuable resource to their school and knowing that they should be directly involved in their child's education, we are requesting each parent to select five areas of service. Please number your selections from 1 to 5, with 1 being your first choice. If you need further details on each area, please call the school.

Father	Mother	
____	____	Class sponsor and room parents
____	____	Volunteer aide
____	____	Vocational and professional week presenter or helper
____	____	Resource and media center aide
____	____	Planning field trips
____	____	Chapel presentations
____	____	Fund-raising
____	____	Historian
____	____	Booster club
____	____	Hospitality to new school families
____	____	Parent visitation
____	____	Library committee
____	____	Making teacher resource materials
____	____	Helping with a.m. or p.m. playground supervision
____	____	Typing, filing, general office help
____	____	Presenting a parent workshop (Area____________)
____	____	School plays and drama
____	____	Transportation coordinator
____	____	Car pooling
____	____	Working at basketball and other games
____	____	Helping coach: Sport ____________
____	____	Fun fair worker
____	____	Tutoring in subject area ____________
____	____	Intercessory prayer leader
____	____	Workday
____	____	Housekeeping/cleaning
____	____	Parent newsletter
____	____	Yearbook assistant
____	____	Help at registration
____	____	Bus loading supervision
____	____	Soup label collections
____	____	Cafeteria supervision
____	____	Hallway monitor
____	____	After school supervision

Printed parent name

Address City Zip

Phone: Home Work

FIGURE 20 - Parent Ministry Survey

senting each grade level are appointed by the pastor and administrator.

Show Appreciation

Express appreciation to all who serve. Appreciation requires admiration, discernment, sensibility, taste, gratitude and esteem. There is no substitute for a face-to-face "well done" declaration to the parent.

Parents (and others who volunteer) need to know you believe in their efforts and sacrifices of time and energy. Assure them their presence is having an eternal effect upon the lives of the students.

In addition to a one-on-one meeting with the parent, consider the following gestures of appreciation:

1. Encouraging students to send special cards (in addition to birthday).
2. Greeting them at the front door.
3. Holding a special parent appreciation assembly.
4. Honoring them on their birthday.
5. Inviting them out to lunch or to a special coffee or tea.
6. Invitation to return next year for further service.
7. Remembering their anniversary.
8. Special name badge.

Give Special Recognition

Showing recognition is important. Be consistent and include all parents, regardless of how small their involvement. Maintaining accurate records is vital to this recognition process. Some suggestions for special recognition might include the following:

1. Scholarships to special seminars.
2. Cafeteria discount cards.
3. Certificates of appreciation.
4. Discounts at bookstore.
5. Set up a special parent bulletin board featuring different families each month.
6. Set up a Parent of the Month and Parent of the Year program.
7. Pins, gifts, or symbols of achievement.
8. Plaques for years of service, 3, 5 7, and 10 years.

9 Community interest story to local newspaper and television station.

10 Warm fuzzies.

Know Where to Go for Answers

A happy parent is not always the one whose child gets good grades, makes the cheerleading squad, or is voted on the homecoming court; rather, it is the parent who knows who to call when they have questions or concerns about teacher conferences, grades, course of study, schedules, absences, reports cards, transcripts, textbooks, lost but found, fees, activities and special events.

Resolve Challenges When They Arise

Avoid the trap of pretending a problem will go away by ignoring it. Dealing with challenges as soon as possible avoids anger and bitterness becoming a foothold. It also strengthens objectivity of those involved. This will help end the "Do Nothing" headlines transmitted back to family and friends.

Make a commitment to deal with every parent complaint within 24 hours. This sends the message back to the home and community, "The school really cares." The following four suggestions will help prevent challenge situations.

1 **Apply the Master's Master Principle**. This means fostering a staff willing to serve. Paul advocates serving: "**...by love serve one another**" (Galatians 5:13). Administrators and teachers can display love by going out of their way to take care of the needs of students and parents. Love, in turn, covers a multitude of sins (Proverbs 10:12). Staff who are showing love are inevitably attracted by the needs of others. First John 3:17(NAS) says, "**But whosoever has the world's goods, and beholds his brother in need and closes his heart against him, how does the love of God abide in him?**"

2 **Follow through on all promises**. When a student or parent submits a request and the school ignores or neglects it, attitudes of resistance develop immediately. Learn to follow through on matters concerning people.

3 **Follow the Matthew 18 principle**. Going directly to the person who has offended you, or has voiced a problem, whether it be students, teachers, parents, administrators, or other staff, builds trust and confidence. Lack of trust destroys the effectiveness of teachers and administrators. Who wants to go to a school where there is little or no trust?

4 **Be Forgiving**. Following this principle requires the school to walk in forgiveness. Ephesians 4:32 instructs us to be forgiving. Students and parents are supportive of school staff who are forgiving and seeking to restore and bring reconciliation by rebuilding relationships rather than tearing them down, or worse yet, doing nothing to mend hurts. An unforgiving spirit displayed by the school will propel parents and students toward withdrawal.

Obtain Input in Decision Making

Before you decide on a matter, seek input from those who will be affected by the decision. Exercising executive power to implement solutions works better when those who have to implement the solution are involved in the decision.

Student, teacher and parent questionnaires, informal administrator rap times, Parent-Teacher Fellowship, parent-teacher conferences, or a parent "drop-in" hour are helpful activities for gaining input into the decision-making process. For example, if you are thinking about opening an after-school program and requiring teachers to staff the program, then teachers should be involved in the planning.

The best retention strategy is producing satisfied parents and students.

Strengthen Program Elements

6

All that schools do and say become a force for student retention. Everyone and every program associated with the school affects retention efforts. Therefore, each program needs to be the very best it can be.

The most important program is academics. Every effort must be made to have the best academic program possible.

Academics

Parents enrolling their children in a Christian school expect a quality academic program. "There is no excuse for the Christian school to provide a shabby educational program" (Billings, 1978, p. 57). The purpose of academics as well as other aspects of the curricula is the fulfillment of 2 Timothy 3:17, **"That the man of God may be perfect, thoroughly furnished unto all good works."**

Academic Content

Narrowly speaking, a curriculum is the subject area or content matter studied. In its broadest interpretation, it includes everything happening in a Christian school.

Every Christian school should follow a basic content for study. Table 2 illustrates subjects taught at various grade levels.

Your goal should be to build a solid foundation in the basics; i.e., Bible, Reading, Writing, Arithmetic, Social Studies and Science.

Forces, both within and outside the Christian school, influence classroom curriculum decisions. As a result, it is not unusual to find schools in constant curricula turmoil depending upon whose child is not passing, which teacher is assigned to the course, or a change in administration. Guard against curriculum change for

TABLE 2 - Academic Content

Early Elem. K-3	Upper Elem. 3-6
Bible	Bible
Writing	Penmanship
Reading (Phonics)	Language Arts (Spelling, Reading, Grammar)
Arithmetic (Numbers)	Arithmetic
Social Studies	History/Geography
Science	Science
Fine Arts (Music, Art)	Fine Arts (Music, Art)
Physical Ed./Health	Physical Ed./Health
Junior High 7-8	**Senior High 9-12**
Bible	Bible 4 Yrs.
Language Arts/Literature	English 4 Yrs.
Grammar, Spelling, Vocabulary and Writing	Social Studies 3-4 Yrs.
Mathematics	For. Languages 1-2 Yrs.
History /Geography/Civics	Science 2-3 Yrs.
Fine Arts/Music/Art	Math 3-4 Yrs.
Physical Ed./Health	Electives
Other Additions	
Home Economics	
Family Living	
Vocational Education	

the sake of change; institute change only to improve or to meet the needs of students.

The cry from secular educators has been, "We must get back to the basics." Many Christian educators add their voice to the chorus. "Back to the basics" for the Christian educator means back to the divine element in the curriculum, including materials which are Bible-integrated, a Christ-centered view of life, and a release of the influence of the Holy Spirit.

Curriculum Selection

The curriculum you select is dependent upon your educational approach. There are three approaches.

Teacher-Directed Approach

The first is the traditional teacher directed approach. In this situation, the teacher or school plans the content and decides what is to be taught. The teacher becomes the key element in the educational process.

A-Beka Book, and Bob Jones University Press are the two major publishers of teacher-directed curriculums. Developed for Christian Schools, these curriculums are Biblically integrated. Curriculum guides provide for the scope and sequence of graded subject content. The curriculum provides the teacher with a variety of proven methods, suggestions on classroom schedules and goals for each subject.

Using guides saves hundreds of hours of preparation time, they are valuable tools for teacher substitutes and help improve instructional and content accountability. Following the curriculum guides allows those involved in the school to know what is to be taught, when it is to be taught and some of the methods used.

The curriculum guide becomes a valuable resource for the new, inexperienced teacher. Teachers and administrators need to see the curriculum guide as a guide, and allow the teacher flexibility to adjust the lessons according to the needs of the students.

Success in the classroom is dependent on more than just covering the curriculum; success is always a result of a positive interaction among the student, the teacher and the curriculum. Guard against the "Curriculum" becoming an instructional bondage to the students and the teacher. Provide the freedom to the teacher to have her daily lesson ordered by the Holy Spirit.

Independent Study Approach

The second approach is independent study. Many schools select this approach when a school has a limited number of classrooms, or a few students are enrolled in several grades. For example, a school may have 40 students in grades kindergarten through six, with only two classrooms and a limited budget.

In the independent study approach, a teacher administers a standardized diagnostic test. The results tell teachers exactly where to start the student in a particular subject. A series of workbooks form the basis for presenting the curriculum. Success in one workbook leads to the next until the student has successfully mastered the subject content.

Schools employing this approach can improve their effectiveness by employing experienced teachers who can direct the educational process, assure sufficient interaction among the students and encourage listening and note-taking skills.

Principles Approach

There is another approach which has found increasing acceptance over the past few years; it is the Principles Approach. This approach is not a curriculum but rather a methodology.

This methodology centers on researching the Scriptures and any pertinent original documentation, reasoning from this information, recording one's conclusion and relating the conclusions to practical aspects of life.

The Best Approach

So which approach results in greater enrollment? When asked this question, we respond, "Any approach will work to increase enrollment, if you work it." There are many examples of successful schools using each approach.

There are also many schools using a combination of approaches. For example, some teacher-directed schools use independent study materials with students who are self-motivated, who have schedule challenges, or need extra units for graduation.

Schools which have been in existence for several years soon discover curriculum alone does not guarantee success; these schools adapt and adjust approaches to meet the needs of their students.

A good example of this is found at Victory Christian School in Tulsa, Oklahoma, where the A-Beka Phonics/Reading approach has been adjusted to include a linguistic component from the York Reading Program. In addition, the Abundant Life Christian School in Madison, Wisconsin, supplements the A-Beka Language Program with materials from Merrill Publishers. It is not unusual to find an independent study school modifying its curriculum with teacher-directed materials. Other schools, such as Bethany Christian Academy in Baker, Louisiana, are moving toward using the Principles Approach in many of its subjects.

Which curriculum is the best? The one resulting in the school accomplishing its purpose, goals and objectives.

Curriculum Goals and Evaluation

Without goals, a school has no direction for curriculum implementation. We offer the following school-wide measurable goals.

1. 100 percent of the students know Jesus Christ as their personal Savior.

2. 100 percent of the students receive a rating of 3 or higher on a 5 point scale as it relates to fruit of the Spirit and character.

3. 100 percent of the students are at grade level as measured by standardized tests.

4. 100 percent of the student body are actively involved in their children's or youth group.

In addition, each course and grade level should have specific goals and objectives, a completed scope and sequence, as well as a method of ongoing evaluation. Different practices in evaluation and reporting exist from school to school - percentage marks, national standardized tests, letter grades, rating scales, pass/fail, criterion referenced tests, narrative reports, checklists, self-reports.

Your Christian school needs to select those methods that best fulfill the purpose of evaluation - providing feedback concerning achievement of classroom and school goals. The evaluation information provides the basis for making individual and institutional decisions to improve education.

Every Christian school should administer a national standardized achievement test. The results should not only be used to compare your school to national norms, but to compare your school with the norms established for other Christian schools. Check with Christian school organizations, such as ACSI

(Association of Christian Schools International) and ORUEF (Oral Roberts University Educational Fellowship) for a summary of Christian school test data.

The following pointers will help improve the effectiveness of your evaluation program.

1 **Don't allow your testing program to become an end in itself**; go beyond the grade equivalent scores and look to see how students are doing on mastery of skills. Are they developing to their full potential?

2 **Be consistent**. Establish a standardized grading system for your school. This will help reduce inconsistences between grades. What really is an **A**'s worth of learning in Mrs. Smith's English class compared to Mr. Jones' English class? Does one teacher give an open book final in World History and another teacher a comprehensive essay test?

3 **Require teachers to produce detailed course syllabi**. Give these to students and parents at the start of each course. Include in the syllabi a listing of unit objectives. Teachers should be able to provide a list of learning objectives.

4 **Establish school-wide homework policies**. This is especially important at the high school level. An average of 15-20 minutes per subject is reasonable.

5 **Provide opportunities for students to make up missed work or to improve their test scores**. This is especially important in subjects where future learning is dependent upon prerequisite information or skills. Students need to know what they have not learned that will cause trouble in subsequent chapters, units, or courses.

6 **Work with parents to help improve student grades**. Many parents suffer from low-grade infection - every time they see their son's report card they get sick.

7 **Help students visualize success**. Jesus helped His disciples visualize success when He said,

> **"Verily, verily, I say unto you, He that believeth on me, the works that I do shall he do also; and greater works than these shall he do . . ."** (John 14:12).

In educational terms, Jesus' works became a self-fulfilling prophecy. Research has established the fact: "Teachers who set and communicate high expectations to all their students obtain greater academic performance from those students than teachers who set low expectations" (U.S. Department of Education, 1986, p. 32).

8 **Redirect negative comments.** Move students to an "I-can-do attitude." Jesus inspired His disciples to expect to do greater things than He Himself had accomplished. We need to instill this same attitude. Guard against telling students how hard and difficult the course content or test will be, giving "trick" questions on tests, or pointing out how few students do well.

For more information on testing and grading see, *The Proper Use of Standardized Tests, Subjective Testing and Grading* and *Classroom Testing* published by Bob Jones University Press.

Strengthen Instruction

Schools desiring to be successful in retaining students must spend quality time in strengthening instruction.

Employ Experienced Teachers

The real key to curricula success rests with the teacher. You can place a superior curriculum in the hands of a less than adequate trained teacher, and your results will be less than optimal.

On the other hand, you can take a curriculum that from outward appearance may not look very promising, but when placed in the hands of a skillful teacher, the curriculum will be successful. What are we saying? Teacher selection is critical to the success of any curriculum.

Furthermore, the teacher is a "LIVING CURRICULUM." The life of a teacher is an open book read by all pupils whether it be in the classrooms or in the shopping center (2 Corinthians 3:2-5). Students need to see the teacher as a consistent example.

Gene Garrick, Pastor of the Tabernacle Church in Norfolk, Virginia, commented (Lowrie, 1978),

> "The influence on students is not just in the classroom, but in the total life of the teacher's attitudes, habits,

character, associations, interests, priorities, motivations, reactions and relationships" (Foreword).

Require of your teachers a commitment to a 24 hour lifestyle. Schindler and Pyle (1979) said,

> "It's how the teacher responds to his own life situations that will be transmitted to the students. It's how the teacher handles his problems, his heartaches, his sins, his mistakes, and those people that despitefully use him, that is what is learned by the students" (p. 46).

Experienced staff who are excited about life in general and the Gospel in particular, have a positive focus on academics and use attractive curricula, will build enrollment.

Provide Necessary Instructional and Resource Materials

Asking a teacher to achieve curriculum goals means making available the necessary materials and resources. Help reduce financial pressure facing teachers by providing all essential classroom supplies. Estimates indicate teachers spend $150 per year out of their own pockets on classroom supplies.

We recommend schools provide an annual classroom budget of $100 - $200 per teacher for these materials. If this in not possible, increase your tuition to cover the expense.

Maximize Use of Time and Resources

Protect instructional time so there are as few interruptions as possible. Avoid excessive public address announcements. Five minutes per period of unprotected instructional time accumulates to three weeks of lost time in an academic year.

Parallel Public School Scope and Sequence

This is especially critical at the high school level. There is nothing more frustrating for a high school student (e.g, Junior) than to transfer to a Christian school and find out the state-required World History is offered at the freshman level, drivers education can only be taken in the summer, Algebra II is a sophomore course and a fourth year of science isn't offered.

Teach All Subjects Well

The Green Bay Packers domination of football in the 60's was based on the explicit execution of a few basic plays. So it is with your school. Concentrate on the basics, then add electives as the school grows. Hire teachers who know their subjects and can teach them well.

Improve Teaching Methods and Activities

Students' perception of teaching methods and activities and their relations to learning can be measured through instruments like the "Classroom Environment Scale" (Moos and Trickett, 1974).

Often, what happens is schools assume their methods and materials are effective as long as their students score at grade level based on standardized testing. Schools can gain a greater insight into these areas by assessing how students feel about what is happening in the classroom.

Two out of the nine subscales of the Classroom Environment Scale measure the extent to which students have attentive interest in class activities and participate in class discussion as well as measuring the amount of unusual and varying activities and assignments planned by the teacher. The instrument assesses the extent to which the teacher attempts to use new techniques and encourages creative thinking.

When Victory administered this assessment, a significant relationship was evidenced between the amount of variety in the classroom and the students' rating of teachers as being a "good teacher." Those teachers receiving a high rating were also the ones providing more involvement and innovation in the classroom.

Overall, the assessment pointed out the need for teachers to use new techniques and activities. The results prompted the teachers during their planning to ask the question, "What am I going to do in class today?" rather than, "What am I going to tell the students today?"

Creativity and innovation in the classroom can be fostered by providing teachers with adequate plan time, professional development activities and opportunities for teachers to share the unique happenings in their classroom. As part of your staff development program or staff meetings, provide an opportunity for teachers to "Share an Idea" (See Figure 21).

Share an Idea

Date ________________

Sharing Teacher ________________

Title of Idea Shared ________________

Objective of the idea: ________________

Materials Needed: ________________

Procedures: ________________

Method of Evaluation: ________________

FIGURE 21 - Share an Idea

Seek Accreditation

Accreditation is viewed as a process whereby an outside, impartial, independent agency conducts a realistic and comprehensive review of a school. The accrediting agency determines a school's ability to meet standards common to schools and to determine objectively the degree to which a school is accomplishing what it is trying to do. To be credible means to believe or trust. "Accreditation, therefore, acknowledges an institution's credibility - its believability. Although some might see an accrediting agency as giving credibility to an institution, in actuality, the process of accreditation ascertains and acknowledges the institution's credibility by providing external witnesses" (Petry, 1989, p. i).

Advantages

There are several distinct advantages of accreditation:

1 It increases the confidence level of parents. Parents equate accreditation with a "good school."

2 It enhances the reputation of the school in the Christian and non-Christian community.
3 It increases the morale of teachers, administration and students.
4 It forces schools to meet objective standards that normally would not have been considered.
5 It leads to upgrading all aspects of the school program.

Bill McCrea, administrator of Community Christian School in Mineral Wells, Texas, commented:

> "Accreditation brings a deep sense of accomplishment. It strengthens the self-image and confidence of each individual involved. It builds a confidence in the school within the community. It insures that each student who passes through its doors will have a better opportunity for success in the post-secondary level and life in general"(ORUEF 1991, p. 5).

Accreditation is welcomed as long as it does not compromise convictions and it aids in confirming the accomplishment of the school's vision. Oral Roberts University is a good example. The university has maintained its accreditation status because of the vision of sending teachers into "every person's world with a message of healing, wholeness and abundant living." Most states will not issue a teaching certificate if the teacher has not graduated from an accredited school. Many of these teachers would be unable to fulfill this vision if ORU did not have an accredited teacher education program.

The Accreditation Process

The accreditation program provided by ICAA allows an opportunity for schools, large, small, new, or established, to progress through a quality assurance program with the goal of excellence.

ICAA's accreditation process involves a progress through three levels.

The first level is Candidacy Status. A school can achieve this status by:

1 Sending a letter to ICAA pursuing the quality assurance process.
2 Becoming a bona fide member of the Oral Roberts Educational Fellowship (ORUEF).
3 Submitting the candidacy survey.

ICAA Commission on Accreditation approves candidacy status. Candidacy status means a school is serious about quality, and under the guidance of ICAA, wants to develop excellence in all areas.

The second level is Provisional Status. This means a school has begun the process of becoming the finest school possible under God's guidance and with the support of ICAA. Schools receive provisional status when at least two staff members have attended the quality assurance seminar, and completed all procedures outlined in the requirement provisions of the accreditation handbook. ICAA commission awards provisional status following a successful review by the ICAA commission and approval of the delegate assembly.

Schools receive Accreditation Status, the highest level, following a recommendation made by a site visitation team, review by the Commission and approval by a Delegate Assembly.

Even if a school does not seek accreditation, the accreditation standards are an excellent plan for developing the school in years to come.

Christian schools participating in and achieving accreditation have a greater opportunity of attracting and retaining students.

Schools interested in accreditation should contact those agencies for more information, whether it be via state or a private Christian agency, such as ACSI, ICAA, or CSI (Christian Schools International).

Parent Credibility

Ultimately, parents are the ones who provide the final test of credibility. If a school is doing a good job, a school will continue to grow; if not, enrollment will steadily decline.

It is good to have on file written testimonials from parents attesting to the quality of education received at the school. In addition:

1 Provide college selection information (post a listing of the names of post high school institutions the school's graduates have attended).
2 Offer a wide selection of course offerings, especially upper division courses.
3 Require student participation in SAT and ACT testing.
4 Accurately identify student G.P.A. and class standing.
5 Make available to high school students college placement services.
6 Deliver the kind and quality of services publicized.

If the school says attending the school will result in higher academic test scores, then this needs to happen. If it says it will provide special programs for children with learning disabilities, or maintain a pupil-teacher ratio of one to twenty, then the school needs to do this. If not, the school is jeopardizing its credibility in the community. Even more importantly, a school is at risk to litigation for breach of contract. Handbooks and documents should contain only those statements concerning implied services and performance the school can deliver.

Athletics

"The inclusion of athletics in the education program of a Christian high school (and elementary school) is expected: parents expect it, students expect it and most educators expect it. Athletics probably contribute more to 'school spirit' than any other single factor" (Churda, 1984, p. 157).

Presently, Victory Christian School has more than 40 sport teams from grades kindergarten through high school. Victory's policy is to offer any sport as long as it meets the following criteria:

1 There are enough students to field a team.
2 There are necessary facilities for practice.
3 There are sufficient financial resources to set up and sustain the sport.

Regardless of how large an athletic program your school has, the conduct of the players and coaches, facilities, uniforms, equipment, scope of program, and level of participation are critical contributions to student retention.

The following suggestions will help you increase the effectiveness of your athletic program.

Promote A Christ-Centered Philosophy in Athletics

Claude Schindler, Pancheco Pyle and Steve Karnehm (1981) have written an excellent resource book for Christian schools.

They recommend the following philosophy of athletics:

> "The Christian approach to athletics must stem directly from the school's Christian philosophy of education, since it is foundational to everything done in the school system. A brief philosophical statement of athletics could be to develop the spiritual part of the athlete so that the Holy Spirit is in control and directing his mind and body" (p. 4).

Expand the Sports Offered

Given adequate facilities, consider hosting a city-wide summer volleyball, basketball, or other sports league. This activity will bring prospective students on campus.

Sponsor a Summer Fun Program

This program works best for children grades 1 - 6 and has the added benefit of providing an exciting day-time placement for working parents.

When school starts in the fall, the chance of enrolling students from these programs is greatly enhanced, especially for parents and students who have had a rewarding experience.

Establish a no-cut policy for all athletic teams unless restricted by association rules. This increases the number involved, allows for further development of skills (many students give up on any further involvement in a particular sport when cut from a team) and causes students who are in starting positions to work harder to maintain these positions.

Evaluate the Athletic Program

Provide a comprehensive evaluation of coaches and programs (A specially-designed evaluation instrument is available from the authors). Use the information obtained from students, coaches, teachers and parents to strengthen your athletic program.

Other Programs

Student Activities

Student activities are a positive attraction for students, especially those in junior and senior high school. Some schools try to justify a less-than-adequate extracurricular activities program by saying, "We don't want to major on the minors," or "We don't want to have a strong athletic program since it will take away from our academics." Activities are going to happen in any school. They can be either planned or unplanned. It is to your advantage to plan for these activities so they can be a positive recruiting and retention tool.

Establish A Master Activities Calendar

In doing so, consider other activities planned by the ministry or community. Avoid as many conflicts as possible by using an activity request process (See Figure 22). Schools with computers would do well to invest in a software package entitled *Creative Calendar Plus* from Powerup, P.O. Box 7600, San Mateo, CA 94403. This program is very simple to operate, yet very effective in scheduling events and producing weekly, monthly and yearly calendars.

Provide a Wide Variety of Activities

In selecting activities, look for ones to enrich and reinforce the philosophy of the school. Offer a variety of activities one to three days a month, such as arts and crafts, in-depth academic activities, science exploration, model building, library club, stamp collecting, etc. Other effective activities are fun fairs, academic olympics, chess-checker tournaments, spirit week, spiritual life council, model building, treasure hunt, hobby day, science scavenger search, secret friend day, record breaking day, egg drop, paper chaining, mural painting, international dinner, school wide talent show and frog racing.

Encourage Maximum Student Participation

Enhance attendance by scheduling some activities during the school day. This allows students with out-of-school obligations and interests to attend. It also alleviates the challenge of students

REQUEST TO SCHEDULE EVENT
ON MASTER CALENDAR

MC# ________

Event Title ________________________________

Section 1: Time Frames

	A	B	C	D	E	F
Day						
Date						
Start Time						
Finish Time						

(Attach Sheet If Space Provided Insufficient.)

Section 2: Facilities

Do you anticipate using ministry facilities? ___ Yes ___ No

If yes, attach Facilities Requisition and indicate room requested ________

If no, explain ________________________________

Section 3: Advertising

Please indicate the means of advertising you plan to use to promote the events.

		Dates From	Dates Thru
Printed:			
	Brochure		
	Church Announcements		
	Church Newsletter		
	Magazines		
	Newspaper		
	Signs/Posters		
Non-printed:			
	Radio Spots		
	Television Spots		
	Announcements from the pulpit		

Section 4: Other Services

Please indicate other services you are requesting.

Audio-Visual: Sound Only ___
Master Tape ___
Tape Copies ___
Projection Eq. ___

Other: Childrens Church ___
Counselors ___
Greeters ___
Nursery Services ___
Special Music ___
Special Speaker ___
Ushers ___
Vehicle Use ___
Youth Service ___
________________ ___

Section 5: Persons Responsible

	Telephone
#1:	
#2:	

(Please Print Names Above)

Requested by (Signatures)	Date

Approvals	Date
Entered On Calendar	

VCS #640-10/82

FIGURE 22 - Request To Schedule an Event

who want to participate but must rely on a school or city bus or others to transport them home. If possible, operate a "late bus." Adding an extra period to the school day allows for scheduling of more activities with fewer conflicts.

Add a modular schedule so students with unscheduled time can be rescheduled for participation in activities. In planning student activities, don't overlook elementary and middle schools; they should have activity programs as part of the total school program. Students who become involved in student activities are more likely to continue in those activities, therefore increasing a school's enrollment potential for the next year. Participating in a good activities program gives the student a sense of belonging and being part of a group.

Expand Membership

Double cast for drama and music productions. Write in scenes requiring large numbers of students, or those from previous productions. Increase the numbers for cheerleader squads and pompon clubs. Squads can take turns going to games.

Broaden Intramural Programs

Include in your program a wider variety of activities, such as two person volleyball, table tennis, arm wrestling, etc.

Consider Off-Campus Outings

Activities, such as camping, hiking, canoeing, horseback riding, hayride, visiting museums, or wilderness outings provide opportunities for students and staff to get to know each other as well as providing good wholesome fellowship for students. The excitement and relationships established during these types of activities help retain students and give them something to talk to their friends about. This indirectly draws them into the group and encourages enrollment.

Organize a winter olympics program, both for academics and physical fitness.

Participating in national competition finals with 1,400 other high school students creates an excitement unsurpassed by any other activity.

New Student Reception

Increase the retention of new students by conducting a monthly new student reception. This is especially important for those students who enter school after school has started and have not attended your new student orientation. The reception will provide an opportunity for establishing friendships. Hold the reception the last period of the day. Consider giving each new student a special surprise packet; include a free lunch ticket, coupons from area merchants, school pencil, etc.

When a new student enrolls, provide each of his/her teachers with a new student data sheet (See Appendix F).

Other Suggestions

The following suggestions will strengthen your activities programs, resulting in greater success in recruiting and retaining students.

1 **Arrange for activities low in cost.** No activity should be so expensive it prohibits attendance. Using a "come one, come all" philosophy will help keep costs to a minimum.

2 **Select motivated sponsors.** Select activity sponsors who enjoy the activity. Assigning advisory responsibilities to those who lack motivation will detract from the effectiveness and value of an activity.

3 **Include adequate supervision.** Use a ratio of one adult to fifteen students. Get parents involved in the planning and supervision.

4 **Properly communicate activities.** It is very rewarding for parents and students to know the who, what, when, where and why of student activities. They should also be able to call the school office and find someone who knows what is happening. Maintaining a master activity log at the receptionist desk would be a great benefit to all concerned. Require a daily posting of activities and updating of changes. For after school hours, consider using a voice message machine giving the times and locations of all after-school activities. Use a machine whereby coaches can call in and record game scores.

5 **Promote friendliness.** Use student activities as a recruiting tool by encouraging students to bring a friend. Sponsor a Bring A Friend Day, Secret Friend Day, Your Custodian is Your Friend Day and Cafeteria Workers are Your Friends Day.

Field Trips

Such aspects as courtesy of students, conduct, attitude and responsibility of students build a reputation affecting recruitment efforts. Institute an effective evaluation system for all field trips (See Appendix G).

Fine Arts, Music, Art and Drama

Participation in city, regional, and state contests are important ingredients in retention. It is not winning that counts, but how students and staff conduct themselves, their attitudes, the life of Christ in them and the selection of material presented. Consider expanding and forming additional groups. The more students you involve in these groups, the greater will be the influence upon the community.

Graduations

Graduation is the single most important event of the year, whether it be kindergarten, 8th grade or high school. It is the one opportunity for parents to see how they have been spending all of their money. It honors God, student success and achievement. It is also the one event that attracts the most community interest. All of the pageantry created by a well run, emotionally and spiritually positive graduation ceremony, has a lasting influence on student recruitment and retention.

When planning, consider the following:

1 **Consider details**. Reducing all details to writing reflects the importance of the event.

2 **Equalize the work**. Spread out the work load among a few dependable staff rather than leaving all the work to a single person. Key elements include: field and stage organization, coordination with music department, organization of processional, appointment and placement of Junior Marshals; arrangement for traffic control; appointment of ushers and ticket takers (in schools with limited space), alternate indoor arrangements in the event of inclement weather; reception following the graduation; special awards; preparation of graduation lists; printing of programs; arrangement for caps and gowns for students, staff and special guests; presenting and distribution of diplomas.

3 **Prepare for questions**. Despite all the practice and planning, there will be hundreds of inquiries. Prepare to take an extra hundred phone calls just before graduation. Consider publishing a graduation guide containing answers to the most frequently asked questions. Include as a minimum: information

about the time; place; inclement weather; tickets; make-up work; special attire; wearing of tassels; reception; pictures; school tuition indebtedness; issuing of diplomas; and returning caps and gowns.

School Newspaper

The daily, weekly, or monthly newspaper is a valuable tool for building school unity. The newspaper brings students, parents and staff in closer contact with one another. Improve the effectiveness of your newspaper by:

1 **Feature special stories.** Include features on school life, hobbies and interests of students and staff. Provide written accounts of notable accomplishments of students and alumni, and use good cartoons on the lighter side of school life; all of these stimulate interest in the school.

2 **Increase circulation.** Obtain permission to distribute your school newspaper to other church youth groups. Add overprints of the newspaper as part of your recruiting literature (packet). Place copies in neighborhood businesses remembering always to enclose a response section in the newspaper.

Everyone and every program associated with the school affects retention efforts. Therefore, every program needs to be the very best it can be!

7

Enhance Ancillary Services

Christian schools need to provide as many services to its parents and students as possible. Food services, health services, library services, pupil personnel services and transportation are all within the capability of any Christian school. The degree to which services function smoothly and operate efficiently will influence the degree to which Christian schools attract and retain students.

Food Services

Most students attending Christian schools eat lunch at school. Schools must view the food service program as a direct influence upon student enrollment.

Our son attended a college weekend sponsored by a private college. When he returned home, we asked how he liked the college. His very first response was, "The food was terrible. If they expect students to eat that kind of food, I'm not interested in attending."

Cafeteria Atmosphere

Not only is good food critical to a student's perception of school, many view a good cafeteria as being a very important part of the day. It is an opportunity to socialize, get the latest school news, find out what everybody is doing and make new friends. A well-managed lunchroom full of happiness, joy and the spirit of caring, leads to high morale and greater enrollment.

It is not necessary for a school to have a hot lunch program. In fact, few schools provide a full-scale hot lunch program; they may have the students bring their lunch and sell milk or juice for a beverage. However, if your school has adequate facilities, provide nutritional and tasty prepared food at the lowest possible cost.

Good Management and a Good Cook are Essential

The key is to fix nutritional foods children like and will eat. Plan on serving a "type A" lunch, a meal consisting of lean meat or an alternative, two or more vegetables or fruit, whole grain or enriched bread or an alternative and fluid milk.

Experience has shown lunch type meals, like tacos, hamburgers, french fries, pizza, spaghetti, hot dogs and sloppy joes served with chips are favorites. Fruit and vegetables are a special hit. Offer a single plate lunch or just a single sandwich item at different prices for elementary and secondary students.

Open or Closed Campus

Should the school observe "open" or "closed" lunch periods? Making this decision may depend on the amount of space available. If you enroll 100-300 students, you need 1,000 to 3,000 square feet in the general eating area, 250 to 600 square feet in the kitchen area and 60 to 80 square feet for storage.

If space is an issue, you may choose to consider staggered lunch periods with about one-third of the students eating at one time. The key is to have unhurried eating to allow students to digest their food properly. When possible, provide for separate elementary and secondary lunch periods.

The "open" campus lunch period is a very strong enrollment attraction for students. In offering an open campus program, reserve the privilege for juniors and seniors. Students should be required to obtain written parental permission and sign out each day. Figure 23 provides an example of an Off-Campus Lunch Pass Agreement.

To increase the benefit of an "open" campus, allow freshmen and sophomores to go off campus one time per month, provided they obtain written permission from parents. Permit junior high students to eat off campus with their parents.

Schools can expand the influence of their food service program by providing banquets for senior citizens, volunteers, singles; an after-service youth snack bar; stewardship banquets; fund-raising dinners; mother/daughter and father/son dinners, etc.

OFF-CAMPUS AGREEMENT

I understand the following conditions are in effect regarding off-campus lunch privileges, and I agree to abide by these regulations.

A student assigned a lunch pass must have the pass renewed at the beginning of each nine-week grading period.

Only those students with a validated lunch pass may leave campus with other students who have lunch passes. All students who leave campus must have a lunch pass in their possession.

Students are to sign out in the school office before leaving and sign in upon returning. Students going off campus for lunch will have their lunch pass revoked if they fail to return on time for classes.

Off-campus lunch passes are available only to students who are in grades 11 and 12; they must also maintain a grade point average of 3.0 or better.

Any student receiving two D's or one F at the mid-quarter grade check or quarter grade check will have their off-campus lunch privilege revoked until the next grade check.

Absolutely no guests are permitted to accompany a student home without written parental permission.

Remember, off-campus lunch passes are subject to the final approval of the principal and may be revoked at any time should it be in the best interest of the student and/or school.

I have read the conditions for off-campus privileges and fully realize that a violation of one or more of them will result in cancellation of my lunch pass.

DATE STUDENT'S SIGNATURE

DATE PARENT'S SIGNATURE

VEHICLE REGISTRATION

Make of Car Model TAG #

Grade point average

Grading Quarter

School Offical Approval Date

FIGURE 23 - Off Campus Agreement

Other Suggestions

The following suggestions will help improve existing food service programs:

1 **Adjust the lunchroom physically**. Paint wall murals. Involve the Parent-Teacher Fellowship in a project to purchase some drapes and new furniture. Replace long gang tables with smaller ones. Create an outside eating area for use in good weather. Install sound-deadening acoustical panels.

2 **Formulate a noon-hour activity program**. Consider providing an opportunity for a different sports experience for students in the gym each week. Schedule club meetings and other activities over the noon hour.

3 **Assure proper supervision**. Adequate supervision of the lunchroom and its facilities during lunch periods is essential, not only for establishing order, but for reducing liability. Remember, control should not be so tight as to stifle the flow of joy and enthusiasm among the students and staff.

4 **Provide eating opportunities**. Allow teachers and students to eat together in a special area of the building for a special occasion; e.g., birthdays, organization meetings, class officers, etc. This helps to reduce the need for supervision and affords an opportunity for students to get to know one another in a less formal setting.

5 **Enlist the aid of others**. Groups, such as student government and service groups, can assist in keeping the lunchroom clean.

6 **Vary the school lunch schedule**. Make it possible so the lowest number of students are in the lunchroom at one time.

7 **Decrease length of lines**. Make every effort to decrease length of lines and other delays at the cafeteria.

8 **Form a menu-planning team**. Invite students to be part of this team.

9 **Consider special meals**. Start a breakfast program and encourage parents and teachers to eat together. Invite special guests; e.g., grandparents, seniors, alumni, businessmen, pastors, parents, etc. Plan a monthly staff breakfast.

10 **Drop all unenforceable lunchroom rules.** Devise ways to enforce those remaining in an unobtrusive, routine manner. The school lunchroom should not be a situation that creates problems.

11 **Begin a "We're blessed with Our Cafeteria" publicity campaign.** Use posters, school paper articles, class meetings, and assemblies.

12 **Ask for suggestions.** Periodically, solicit student and staff suggestions about the school's food service program.

Health Services

Parents involved in the medical and health service professions will be looking for a school displaying a strong health service program. Parents view school health services as an important adjunct to the program of the Christian school.

The health service program is to help students develop their body, mind and spirit. Walking in divine health is to be a way of living designed to help students achieve well-being in four areas: nutrition, physical awareness, stress reduction and self - responsibility. Training students to declare God's Word of healing and wholeness for their body is a critical ingredient to the school's health program.

The following suggestions are made to strengthen your health services program:

1 Set up specific measurable objectives.

2 Communicate these objectives to students, parents, faculty and administrators.

3 Provide written job descriptions and expectations for health personnel.

4 Allow for periodical supervision and evaluation throughout the school year.

5 Make school health personnel accessible to students, parents, faculty and administrators.

6 Meet the health needs of the students.

7 Keep up-to-date health records (See Figures 24).

8 View the services as a valuable adjunct to the total school program.

VICTORY CHRISTIAN SCHOOL STUDENT HEALTH RECORD

(To be filled out by the private physician)

MEDICAL EXAMINAION

Date ________
Height ____ *Weight* ____ *B.P.* ____
Speech Problem ____
Nutrition and general appearance ____
Skin ____ Glands ____
Eyes ____ (Indicate test technique)
Vision L. 20/ ____ Both ____
Vision R. 20/ ____
Ears L. ____ R. ____
Hearing L. ____ R. ____
Nose ____
Throat ____
Teeth ____
Thorax ____
Heart ____
Lungs ____
Abdomen ____
Extremities ____
Posture ____
Emotional adjustment ____
Allergy ____

PHYSICIAN'S RECOMMENDATIONS

Any Restrictions (Physical Education or Sports) ____
If yes, please explain ____
Date ____
Physician's Signature ____

RECEIVED DENTAL CARE

Date ____
Dentist's Signature ____

VISION AND HEARING SCREENING

	Date	L	R
Pre-School Vision Clinic			
Professional			
Pre-School Hearing Clinic			
Professional			

Reverse side of this card should be filled in by the parents.)

STUDENT HEALTH RECORD—TO BE FILLED IN BY PARENTS

Name ____ Birth Date ____
Address ____ Home Phone ____
School ____ Grade ____ Section ____
Parent's Name ____ Bus. Phone ____
Child's Physician ____ Phone ____
If your doctor has ordered regular medication for your child, what is it's purpose? ____
List any known allergies your child may have ____

Is your child subject to any of the following? (Indicate if occasional or frequent.)

Colds ____ Headaches ____
Coughs ____ Dizziness ____
Asthma ____ Recurring injury ____
Hay Fever ____ Bed Wetting ____
Shortness of Breath ____ Does he/she tire easily? ____

	DATE		DATE		DATE		DATE
Chicken Pox		Whooping Cough		Pneumonia		Serious accidents	
Measles (Rubeola)		Strep throat		Tonsillitis		Fractures	
Measles (Rubella)		Meningitis		Ear infections		Surgery	
Mumps		Encephalitis		Diabetes		Allergies	
Scarlet Fever		Mononucleosis		Rheumatic fever		Seizure disorder	

Other Illness or Operations ____

FIGURE 24- Health Card

9 Make use of community health service resources.

10 Organize school health services to meet health objectives.

11 Encourage students to participate in health and safety clubs.

12 Locate the health services in an area carefully planned so students can be properly treated in an expedient fashion. Some-

ACCIDENT REPORT

Date: ____ Time: ____

Name: ____ Age/Grade: ____

Place of Accident: Sch. Bldg.____ Sch. Grounds____ To or from Sch..____ Home____
Athletic Trip.____ Town ____ State____

Possible nature of injury:
Abrasion____ Fracture____
Bite____ Foreign Obj. in eye____
Bleeding____ Laceration____
Broken Teeth____ Puncture____
Bruise____ Scratch____
Burn____ Shock(El.)____
Concussion____ Sprain____
Dislocation____ Strain____
Other (Specify)____

Part of body injuried:
Ankle L-R____ Foot L-R____
Arm L-R____ Hand L-R____
Back____ Head____
Chest____ Knee L-R____
Ear L-R____ Leg L-R____
Elbow L-R____ Mouth____
Eye L-R____ Nose____
Finger____ Tooth____
Other____

How did accident happen? What was the student doing? Where was student? List specifically unsafe acts and unsafe conditions existing. Specify any tool, machine or equipment involved.

____

____

____

____

First-aid treatment? Yes____ No____ If yes, by whom?____
Student sent to: School Nurse____ Home____ Doctor____ Hospital (Name)____

How sent? (Car, Ambulance, other) ____

How was the parent notified? ____ When?____

Name of individual notified____ When?____

By whom? ____ Witnesses ____

Where did the accident happen(Specific location)?____

Remarks ____

____

____

Signed: Teacher in charge:____

Principal____ Superintendent ____

FIGURE 25 - Accident Report

one must oversee this area carefully, and in the event of an emergency, assigned personnel must know what to do.

13 Keep proper documentation on all injuries (See Figure 25).

14 Expand duties for health service staff to include checking on physical education excuses in the morning.

Keep current on the communicable diseases in the school population, safety and hazards in the building and on the campus and communications concerning health issues and health education to the staff, students and parents.

15 Offer special programs on sex education, AIDS, drugs, eating disorders and preventative hygiene.

Library Services

Schools with a quality library stand a better chance of attracting and retaining students. Every school can have a quality library. All it takes is a little planning.

The purpose in establishing a library is to glorify the Lord Jesus Christ, consequently support and complement the courses taught in the school's curriculum and aid in the improvement in reading. The library provides the opportunity for quality Christian recreational reading. It also introduces students to the rich heritage of edifying Christian literature from various ages and cultures. Finally, it helps the development of library skills.

Staffing

Appoint a teacher or interested parent to help organize the library. Before school opens, obtain the services of a public school librarian to help organize your library. In schools with an enrollment of less than 200 students, employ a teacher with some training in library science or a part-time professional librarian. For schools enrolling 200 to 500 students, employ a full-time librarian.

Materials and Equipment

1 **Arrange for a centralized library**. Under this plan, all library materials can be checked out by anyone in the school. To build your library, contact the public library and public schools. Periodically, old books are taken off the shelves in place of new books. These books are either sold to the public at substantial savings or given away to other educational institutions. Also participate in the public lending library system.

When Victory first opened, an announcement was made for members of the congregation to donate books. Nearly 1,500 volumes were collected the first two weeks. Other schools have built their library by organizing a special library booster club, seeking donations, writing library grants and holding book fairs. David C. Cook Publishing Company has a program called Chariot Book Fair. They send the school a preselected package of best selling books which retail for about $135. For participating, a school may receive up to $65 worth of books free (1-800-323-7543). A second book club is sponsored by God's World Publications P.O. Box 2330, Asheville, NC 28802 (800-476-8924). They offer 600 titles from 80 different publishers. Almost all of the books are half price or even less. They also provide information on how to start a book club.

If space for a central library is not available, you may consider placing books on carts and moving them among the rooms or establish small collections of books in each classroom.

2 **Provide each teacher with a book budget**. Teachers should be able to purchase new books for the classroom to augment the instructional program and provide opportunity for recreational reading by students during spare moments.

3 **Arrange for adequate space**. There should be space enough to seat the largest class in the school, plus around 20 more students. Twenty-five square feet per reader is ideal. Locate the library centrally so it is accessible to the largest number of students. Disconcerting noises should be at a minimum.

4 **Provide for adequate equipment**. Equip every library to meet the needs of staff and students.

5 **Establish a well-balanced book supply**. This should be in sufficient variety and number. Unfortunately, the library in many Christian schools too often has the same old books, ragged, torn, soiled and unattractive. They stay on the shelves for years. In most cases, they are collections of worn-out texts, unattractive sets, cheap series, undesirable gifts, out of date, and unsuitable to the active needs of students.

Stock the library with up-to-date encyclopedias, dictionaries of words, people, and places, almanacs, current magazines and periodicals. The American Library Association recommends the following (See Table 3):

TABLE 3 - Book Count		
School Enrollment	Number of Titles	Number of Volumes
Up to 200	1700	2000
500	3500	5000
1000	5000	7000

Contact the International Christian Accrediting Association for a listing of suggested titles.

6 **Screen all books.** It is important to review all books for content contrary to the values of the school (See Appendix H). Teachers, librarian, or a committee of concerned parents can perform this task. Thoroughly review each volume since the title may not reflect the contents.

For more information on book reviews, contact the Gabler Foundation and the Association of Christian Schools International.

Environment

Develop a warm, caring environment conducive to learning with frequent access. A well-functioning library could become a hub of the school program. Publish a library usage schedule to assure that each class has an opportunity to visit the library no less than two times each week.

Procedures

Well established procedures allow for maximum utilization of the library resources. Consider the following:

1 **Develop an effective checkout and return system.** Victory Christian School has been granted permission from the publishers of the Dewey Decimal System to change the system to better suit Christian schools. A complete guide to establishing a Christian school library is available upon request from the authors.

2 **Expand the library.** Plan to expand the library into an instructional materials center benefiting the entire ministry.

3 **Start a special collection.** Include pamphlets, bulletin clippings, travel folders, pictures, maps, charts, etc.

4 **Make available audio visual materials.** These should include as a minimum: 16mm projector, overhead projector, filmstrip and slide projector, record player, cassette record player. Add an opaque projector at a later date.

5 **Participate in free films.** A free film program is sponsored by Gospel Films, Inc., P.O. Box 455, Muskegon, MI 49443-0455.

Pupil Personnel Services

If you were to conduct a survey among Christian school administrators and teachers, most would indicate a dissatisfaction with the level of pupil personnel services in their schools. The question is not one of whether or not such services are important; rather, it is primarily a financial issue, providing qualified staff and guidance resources.

Most Christian schools because of their small size, are unable to provide for a full-time guidance counselor. However, schools not meeting the counseling, educational and vocational planning needs of its students, run the risk of losing students and failing to attract parents who are serious about their child's educational future.

Schools without specialized staff can meet student service needs by dividing these responsibilities among available staff.

Regardless of the size of your school, you can have an effective pupil personnel service program. All it takes is a little planning. Consider the following:

1 **Conduct a student survey.** How well are you doing? You will never know unless you ask. Conduct a guidance program checkup using the survey in Appendix I.

Answers to this survey will help identify areas needing improvement. Administer the survey the first year to all high school students, then the following years to graduating seniors.

2 **Conduct a needs assessment.** Asking students to respond to a list of questions provides a simple assessment of the scope of guidance concerns (See Figure 26).

3 **Form a guidance council.** Set up a Guidance Council consisting of staff members representing various areas of the

LETTERHEAD

Former students at Victory Christian School have asked many questions about themselves and the school. You may have some of the same questions. Read each question, then circle the number of the questions you may want to know the answer to.

1. How can I improve my grades?
2. What occupation should I select when out of school or college?
3. What courses should I take next semester and the remaining years of high school?
4. What influence will my abilities, interests and grades mean in terms of my present and future opportunities?
5. Should I continue going to a Christian High School?
6. How do I become a better reader?
7. What can I do to get along better with others?
8. How do I deal with peer pressure?
9. How can I made new friends?
10. Are there any techniques I can learn to help me be more responsible?
11. How can I develop new hobbies and recreational interests?
12. How can I become more like Christ?
13. Should I go to college?
14. If I go to college, where should I go?
15. If I were in college, in what area should I major?
16. How can I find summer work, part time work, or work when I graduate?
17. How can I be a better help in my family?
18. How can I avoid the homework hassle?
19. How can I strengthen my Christian testimony?
20. How can I overcome temptations to lower my Christian standards?

FIGURE 26 - Guidance Survey

school. Include an administrator, counselor, a representative from the social studies department, math and English departments, the school chaplain, an elementary and middle school representative and librarian.

The task of the Council is to administer the guidance survey, tabulate the results, adopt short- and long-range objectives for the guidance program, and recommend in-service activities and guidance resources.

The Council would investigate programs in other Christian school systems which are appropriate for the school. It would also establish guidelines for the ongoing evaluation of the total pupil services program and make recommendations to the administration. Finally, the Council would identify staff members in various positions who would be involved in delivering guidance services.

4 **Develop an anecdotal reporting system**. A school-wide anecdotal reporting system provides a running record of the activities and progress of individual students. The information reported is helpful for program adjustments, public relations and parent-teacher conferences. When correctly used, the system not only pinpoint behavioral challenges, but it is used to report the incidents which portray social, spiritual and academic progress and maturity in the pupils (See Figure 27).

5 **Use computer software**. There are a number of excellent computer software packages for use in college and vocational planning: College Selection Service, Peterson's Guides, Inc., Princeton, NJ 08540; College Explorer, College Board, 45 Columbus Avenue, New York, NY 10023; College Search Program, ACT Program, 230 Schelling Circle, Hunt Valley, MD 21031.

6 **Plan one-on-one conferences**. Plan for at least one personal conference each quarter with every student. Since the junior and senior years are pivotal years for students, plenty of one-on-one academic counseling is advisable.

7 **Present day and evening workshops**. A carefully orchestrated series of day and evening workshops dealing with student and parent concerns will foster retention of students.

Junior High. Orientate parents to curricula offerings and options available. Show 7th graders the benefits of pursuing a foreign language or Algebra 1 in eighth grade. Provide programs on building study and test-taking skills (See Study Power published by The American College Testing Program, 1987).

9th Grade. Conduct a family workshop to plan a four-year high school program. Provide a planning guide, clarify consequences of selecting particular course work and orient

The following are characteristics of a good anecdote:

1. It provides an adequate setting (date, place, and situation).

2. It describes the actions of the child, the reactions of the other people involved, and the response of the child to these reactions.

3. It quotes what is said to the child and by the child during the action.

4. It supplies "mood cues"—postures, gestures, noise qualities, and facial expressions that give cues to how the student felt (not an interpretation of feelings, but objective cues).

5. The description is extensive to cover the episode.

Name: ______________________________

Date: ______________________________

Class/Place: ______________________________

Anecdote: ______________________________

____

____

____

____

____

____

Teacher signature Date

FIGURE 27 - Anecdote Record

parents as to college admissions requirements. Demonstrate college/career computer software.

10th Grade. Encourage accelerated math students to take a sophomore PSAT as practice for the junior year PSAT/NMSQT.

11-12th Grade. Publish and distribute college planning materials. Make available a college scholarship resource file. Provide study resource materials for the PSAT and SAT. Hold a workshop on college financial assistance options. Hold a college fair.

8 **Listen to the Holy Spirit**. The Holy Spirit is the best guidance counselor. Train your students and staff to be sensitive in their spirits to the voice of the Holy Spirit.

Transportation

Most Christian schools are commuter schools; therefore the need for transporting students to and from school is a very real issue. It is not unusual to find parents who are willing to enroll their children providing they can find adequate transportation. Thus, the decision by the school to provide or not to provide transportation is critical.

Schools can opt to own and operate their own transportation services, contract for these services, or lease vehicles. Each option has its own set of advantages and disadvantages.

Operating one or two buses represents a tremendous financial drain upon the school because buses require a high capital investment as well as ongoing costs for maintenance, fuel, insurance and drivers.

Depending upon city and state laws, a school may be eligible for certain tax exemptions in purchasing vehicles, minimum cost for vehicle licenses and reduced insurance rates.

In some states, such as Wisconsin, the state must transport students attending private schools or pay for their transportation.

To strengthen the effectiveness of your transportation program, consider the following:

Keep Costs to a Minimum

It is very difficult to operate a transportation program as a break-even service; you must know your cost per pupil, per mile and per vehicle.

Fees charged for the services are directly related to the number of children needing rides. By taking the cost to operate the vehicles and dividing it by the average number of riders, you will come up with a per pupil cost. Be careful not to under-project these costs. It is not unusual to start the year with a large number of riders, and as the school year progresses, see ridership decline as parents find less expensive means of getting their children to school. It is far better to have a higher fee at the beginning of the year than to increase rates later on in the school year.

Transportation costs can be lessened by carefully selecting routes as well as providing centralized stops rather than door-to-door service.

Using one bus to travel more than one route (multiple routing) is cheaper than a single one, because it allows one bus to provide the services of several. The disadvantage is in the need to stagger dismissal times.

Schools without enough students to merit a bus route might consider a joint venture with other Christian schools in the community.

Your transportation costs should compare favorably with transportation costs in other private schools of similar size.

Minimize Time on Vehicles

Pick up pupils no earlier than one hour before the opening of school; no child should ride longer than one hour at a time. Also, everyone is counting on the vehicles being prompt!

Employ a Quality Driver

As with virtually any type of service operation, the personnel who participate in the program is one of the most important factors in bringing success to the program. In many instances, a bus driver may have more contact with students on a daily basis than the principal.

Avoid the mistake of using the "warm body" method of hiring. A quality bus driver is one of the best public relations agents a school has. How a driver responds to students and parents will have a far-reaching influence upon the transportation program and student retention efforts.

Select drivers who are not only responsive to the desires and concerns of the school, but to those who ride the bus and pay for its services; select those who will be good role models for students, exhibiting Christ-like qualities, and will make the safety of the riders a primary concern.

Provide for a Behavior Code for Riders

An agreed upon set of rules governing the conduct of students should be in place. Permission for any pupil to ride on school vehicles, whether they be bus or van, must be conditioned on good behavior and observing the rules (See Figure 28).

VICTORY CHRISTIAN SCHOOL

SAFETY AND BEHAVIOR CODE FOR BUS RIDERS

PERMISSION FOR ANY PUPIL TO RIDE IN A BUS IS CONDITIONED ON HIS GOOD BEHAVIOR AND OBSERVANCE OF THE FOLLOWING RULES AND REGULATIONS. ANY PUPIL WHO VIOLATES ANY OF THESE WILL BE REPORTED TO THE SCHOOL PRINCIPAL AND CAN BE DENIED PERMISSION TO RIDE A BUS TO AND FROM SCHOOL.

1. The emergency door is not to be opened except at the direction of the bus driver. If the door is open, it could endanger the lives of the passengers.
2. No student is permitted to be out of his seat while the bus is in motion.
3. All students are under the direct control and supervision of the bus driver while on the bus. Obey the driver's suggestions promptly.
4. Students are not to talk to the bus driver while the bus is in motion.
5. Keep all parts of the body inside the bus at all times after entering and until leaving the bus.
6. No food or drink (bottles, canned or otherwise) will be permitted on bus.
7. No seat is reserved or may be held for another student.
8. No one should run toward a school bus while it is in motion.
9. Pupils who must cross the road after embarking from bus should pass in front of the bus at the direction of the bus driver. Pupils are not to cross behind the bus.
10. Follow the dress and honor codes.
11. Keep bus clean.
12. Any complaints by the drivers, pupils or parents should be reported promptly to the principal and/or Transportation Department. (The Transportation Department Phone Number is 663-0675.)
13. Good behavior and manners are expected at the designated bus stop, as well as, on the way to the stop.
14. *Students can be denied perission to ride a bus to and from school.*

RESPONSIBILITIES OF BUS DRIVERS, PRINCIPALS AND PARENTS

1. The bus driver shall be responsible for the conduct of students on his bus. All infractions are to be reported to the principal of the school. The bus driver is authorized to assign seats.
2. It will be the responsibility of all principals to work with the bus drivers on discipline infractions and student suspensions from school buses.
3. All revocations and reinstatement of riding privileges will be handled through the principal.
4. It is also the responsibility of all principals to discuss the *Safety and Behavior Code for Bus Riders* with students and to be sure each student and his parents receive a copy of the code.
5. It is the parent's responsibility to discuss with his child the provisions of the *Safety and Behavior Code for Bus Riders* and to support the principal in the enforcement of the code.
6. The parent must assume responsibility for the behavior of his child while riding the bus. IF PERMISSION TO RIDE THE BUS IS REVOKED, THE PARENT MUST PROVIDE TRANSPORTATION TO AND FROM SCHOOL FOR HIS CHILD UNTIL SUCH TIME AS REINSTATEMENT MAY BE MADE.

THESE REGULATIONS AND LIST OF RESPONSIBILITIES SHOULD BE KEPT BY THE PARENT OR GUARDIAN FOR REFERENCE DURING THE ENTIRE TIME THE STUDENT IS IN SCHOOL.

TO: PARENTS OF CHILDREN RIDING SCHOOL BUSES
FROM: THE VICTORY CHRISTIAN SCHOOL, Transportation Department

Dear Parent:

In order for you to understand and become familiar with the regulations covering the conduct of your child while riding a Victory Christian Bus, as well as your own responsibilities, we are sending you excerpts from SCHOOL BUS TRANSPORTATION, Policies, Regulations and Procedures, pertaining to you. It is requested that you and *your child* read these responsibilities and regulations.

This application will be used as a permanent record throughout your child's enrollment in Victory Christian School. Your cooperation with us will make it possible to provide a *safer* and *more efficient* transportation program.

— PLEASE SIGN AND RETURN TO THE PRINCIPAL IN ORDER FOR YOUR CHILD TO RIDE THE SCHOOL BUS —

FOR JUNIOR & SENIOR HIGH SCHOOL STUDENTS

I have read and understand the regulations and responisbilities of students riding buses and agree, as a passenger, to abide by said regulations.

Student Signature ______________________

Grade ________ School ________

Bus No. ______________________

FOR PARENT OR GUARDIAN OF ALL STUDENTS
Elementary, Junior and Senior High

I have read and understand the regulations and responsibilities of students riding buses and agree to assume full responsibility for my child's conduct on said buses.

Parent or Guardian Signature ______________________

Address ______________________

Date of Application ______________________

(No student will be considered for Transportation privileges until his application has been properly signed and filed with the school.)

FIGURE 28 - Bus Rider Agreement

Providing a behavior code for riders is extremely important since the role of the driver is to operate the vehicle in a safe manner, not to be responsible for disciplining students.

FIGURE 28 - Bus Rider Agreement (Front)

Set up a referral system to effectively deal with disciplinary challenges (See Figure 29). Establish strict standards of safety.

There is no substitute for a strong vehicle safety program, one including in-service training for all drivers, vehicle safety inspections, maintenance schedules and emergency evacuation plans, to name a few.

SCHOOL BUS INCIDENT REPORT TO PARENTS
VICTORY CHRISTIAN SCHOOL
Tulsa, Oklahoma

Date ______________ 19__

DEAR PARENTS:
The purpose of this report is to inform you of a disciplinary incident involving the student on the school bus, which may have jeopardized the safety and well-being of all students.
You are urged to both appreciate the action taken by the driver and to cooperate with the corrective action initiated today by the School District.

______________________________ has been cited for an infraction of the rules listed below:

INFRACTION:

- ☐ Improper Boarding/Departing Procedures
- ☐ Bringing Articles Aboard Bus Of Injurious or Objectionable Nature
- ☐ Failure To Remain Seated
- ☐ Refusing To Obey Driver
- ☐ Fighting/Pushing/Tripping
- ☐ Hanging Out Of Window
- ☐ Throwing Objects In Or Out Of Bus
- ☐ Lighting Matches/Smoking On Bus
- ☐ Spitting/Littering
- ☐ Unnecessary Noise
- ☐ Tampering With Bus Equipment
- ☐ Rude Discourteous And Annoying Conduct
- ☐ Destruction Of Property
- ☐ Other Behavior Relating To Safety, Well-Being And Respect For Others

SPECIFIC DETAILS: ______________________________

PREVIOUS WARNINGS ☐ REPORTED 1ST OFFENSE ☐ REPORTED 2ND OFFENSE ☐ REPORTED 3RD OFFENSE ☐

DISCIPLINARY ACTION TO BE TAKEN: ______________________________

Bus riding is a privilege which may be revoked. Parents are urged to appreciate the disciplinary action taken and to discuss this to prevent further occurrence.

School student is transported to or from	Student's Name	Class-Grade	Date of Incident
	Student's Address	Bus No.	Trip
School	Phone No.	Driver	A.M. P.M.

PRINTED IN U.S.A.
TRADEMARK

PARENT'S COPY

AUTHORIZED SIGNATURE TITLE

FIGURE 29 - Incident Report

Establish a Parent Support Service

Although a school may not offer transportation services, it can play a strong supportive role in helping parents with their transportation needs. Consider providing the following support program.

1 **Locate residences**. Using a large city or county map, pinpoint the location of each family residence.

2 **Streets**. Identify major east-west, north-south streets leading to the school. Draw concentric circles on the map showing one to five mile radiuses.

3 **Driving times**. Calculate driving times from various key points in the city.

4 **Car pools**. Using special identification, indicate those families needing rides and those willing to participate in a car pool.

5 **Zip code coordinators**. Provide a family listing by zip codes along with addresses and phone numbers. Appoint parent zip code coordinators.

6 **Phone call tree**. Establish a phone call tree to notify parents of early or late dismissals, pickups and arrivals due to weather-related conditions or mechanical failures of the school vehicles.

Use Only Well-Maintained Buses

A school bus is a moving billboard. Mechanical breakdowns, driving patterns and parking styles, all influence how people view the school.

For more information and suggestions on establishing an effective Christian school transportation service, see *Christian School Transportation* by the authors.

The degree to which ancillary services function smoothly and efficiently will influence the degree to which Christian schools attract and retain students.

Consider Your Facilities

8

One should not underestimate the influence of the physical condition and general appearance of the school facilities upon recruiting and retention efforts.

Improve Appearance

How many of us have heard the saying, "Don't judge a book by the cover," yet publishing companies spend thousands of dollars designing just the right cover, because covers sell books.

Roy W. Lowrie, Jr. said,

> "When inadequate facilities and equipment are used, the students and teachers will pay the price. There are no short-cuts, even in the Christian school, to quality education. The buildings should not be luxurious, but they must be big enough and designed well enough to allow a top-quality program. No student should have to trade an academic penalty in order to get a Christian education."

When parents at Victory Christian School were asked what prompted them to choose Victory over other Christian schools, 8 percent said they had based their final decision on the quality facilities Victory had to offer.

> "The physical condition and general appearance of school facilities constitutes the basis upon which many citizens make their initial judgment about the quality of the school and the educational program" (Jordon, et. al., 1985, p. 59).

All of us have looked at people who were dirty, poorly dressed and unkept. Failing to pay attention to the outward appearance leads people to question inner motives and attitudes. It shows lack of self-discipline, lack of caring and poor habits. Maintenance of the physical appearance of the building (exterior and interior) is an expression of a school's self-regard and regard for students and staff.

Robert Billings (1978) said, "You don't have to have a million dollar campus, but the campus you rent, buy, or build should project a kingdom image" (p. 59).

Entrances

The most important parts of the building are the exterior entrance and area immediately inside. These must be especially inviting. When parents, students and visitors come through your doors, they need to feel good about what they see.

People entering the building for the first time need to know where to locate various offices, classrooms, etc. (Use plenty of signs where needed.) This sends a positive message to the first time visitor. "Come on in, we were expecting you; let us be of service." Walk through your main entrance. Do you feel invited, welcomed, expected?

Maintenance and Housekeeping

Everyone likes a building which gives evidence of good housekeeping from outside to inside, from trimming the lawn, to dusting off bookshelves. Maintenance and housekeeping may be very time consuming and require a lot of energy, but it is worth the extra effort.

A survey of 53 "showcase" schools in the Houston Independent School District revealed 13 common practices which have seemingly resulted in well-kept buildings and grounds (Hughes and Ubben, 1984, p. 275):

1 Principal (or someone else in supervisory capacity) frequently walks around the building.

2 Litter abatement or housekeeping is discussed at teachers' meetings.

3 Principal sees that each member of the custodial staff has a specific work schedule.

4 Custodial staff sweeps halls regularly during the school day.

5 Custodial staff inspects and cleans restrooms regularly during the school day.

6 Custodial staff are specifically instructed to pick up litter in and around the school on a daily basis.

7 Overall appearance of school is a criterion for evaluating custodial staff members.

8 Student organizations assist in responsibility for keeping the school clean.

9 Parents help maintain or beautify the campus.

10 School newspapers print reminders of neatness, cleanliness, trash pickup and litter control.

11 Students are reprimanded or disciplined for littering.

12 Rules restrict the removal of food and beverages from the cafeteria area.

13 Teachers stress maintaining the environment as part of their regular curriculum.

Develop A Strong Maintenance And Custodial Team

The blessings of increased use of a church building by a Christian day school directly relates to increased custodial and maintenance needs.

A challenge often confronting churches with day schools is who should be responsible for the overall custodial and maintenance program. Since the day school usually occupies the building for the greater part of the time it is open, assign the building principal responsibility for the physical condition and cleanliness of the school plant. However, the principal will need to establish a close working relationship with other users of the building to minimize conflict, such as a Sunday School class leaving coffee cups in the classrooms on Sunday, the youth department re-arranging classroom desks, etc.

Some raise the question, "If the appearance of the building is so important to recruiting and retaining students as well as its effectiveness of learning, would it be better to hire a maintenance and custodial service, rather than doing these duties ourselves?"

Although it is possible for the school to have its own personnel perform many of the custodial functions, some outside professional assistance may be necessary, especially for maintenance. The following are some advantages and disadvantages of contracted maintenance services (Jordon, et. al., 1985, p. 299).

Advantages

1. Employees with specialized skills will be available when needed.
2. Specialized equipment to perform various tasks will be available without large expenditures by the school.
3. Contractors will provide better supervision because of the driving force of the "profit motive."
4. The local school can avoid some of the problems involved in fringe benefits and other personnel programs for employees.
5. Qualified personnel will be available during peak periods, and the school will not be over-staffed when the need no longer exists.
6. Inspection programs will be performed more efficiently because of the binding nature of the contract and specialized qualifications of the contractor's employees.

Disadvantages

1. School maintenance and custodial responsibilities are somewhat unique, and contract personnel may not understand the performance requirements for each task or have a feeling or pride in their work.
2. The support role of custodial and maintenance programs may not be recognized by contract personnel who are not part of the organization and who will not be affected if the total educational program succeeds of fails.
3. The rigid provisions of the contractual relationship may not provide for the flexibility needed to cope with emergency and problem situations that arise.
4. In all likelihood, the school district will be forced to employ some custodial and maintenance personnel though the bulk of the services may be provided on a contract basis; e.g., day custodians and certain classifications of maintenance person-

nel may be employed more economically by the school district than through private contractors.

5 Schedules for contract employees may not be sufficient to make facilities available for after-school use by pupils or community groups.

6 Total operation and maintenance costs may be greater because of role specialization with contract personnel.

The most appropriate approach will vary among schools. One should also consider using students and staff to tend standard end-of-day house-keeping tasks (sweeping floors, taking out the trash, etc.).

How much custodial work there is to do depends upon the standard of cleanliness you desire. There is no easy formula to determine how many hours are needed to maintain a school. Albert S. Prentice (1968) offers a square footage rule of thumb to determine the minimum amount of time required. 14,000 sq. ft. = 8 hrs. of custodial services. Given 36,531 sq. ft., divided by 14,000 sq. ft. = 2.60% x 8 hrs. of custodial services = 21 hrs., 20 minutes. per day. Add to this figure, a five percent accommodation figure for size, shape of room, grade level, flooring, etc., and you have approximately 25 total hours of custodial time. See Appendix J for a listing of special cleaning tasks.

Provide each custodian (teacher, class, etc.) with a written custodial area assignment (See Figure 30).

You may also consider requiring each school family to sign up for a one- or two-hour block, once a month custodial service time. A monthly Saturday cleanup can help grounds maintenance (playground, lawn, parking areas, etc.), minor repairs and detailed cleaning. Volunteers will be more motivated to work when they know exactly what is required of them and have all the necessary equipment and supplies.

Improve student and teacher morale by taking care of maintenance requests in an expedient manner. A simple work request form will help facilitate this task (See Figure 31).

Deal with Vandalism Immediately

Vandalism has a negative effect upon students, staff and parents. When vandalism happens, correct it immediately. Use

TO: ______________________________

Date ______________

You and your classroom have been assigned the following area(S):

Area assigned: ______________________________

Together, we can keep our school building clean and presentable. IFirst Corinthians 14:40 says, "Let all things be done decently and in order."

Each teacher and students are expected to do the best job possible. Your assignment will be easier when you enjoy and receive satisfaction from your work.

REGULAR TASKS REQUIRED IN AREA ASSIGNED

1. Pick up all trash and dump trash in containers located in the custodial closet. Tie all trash bags and place them outside of the classroom.
2. Clean all desk tops; wash if necessary.
3. Erase and wash chalkboards.
4. Vacuum the carpet thoroughly.
5. Turn off all lights, and lock the door when leaving.
6. Report repairs as needed using the standard work order.
7. Report any vandalism to the building principal.

Other Tasks Assigned

____

____

FIGURE 30 - Custodial Assignments

time during holidays to make major improvements in the appearance of your building. The building should be in near-perfect condition when pupils return from vacation.

It takes everyone working together to provide a well-kept, clean building and grounds. Housekeeping can be enhanced by:

- Sponsoring clean-up, pick-up and fix-up days, and enlisting the help of parents, pupils and staff.
- Involving student and parent organizations (e.g., parent-teacher fellowship, student government, booster club, etc.) in raising funds for special building projects, such as a creative play center, garden, fountain, draperies, carpet, etc.

It doesn't matter if your school is a new open space structure, or an eighty-year old traditional structure. As long as it is well-kept, pleasant looking, and well equipped, it will enhance retention.

WORK ORDER

Requested by: ______________________ Date: ________
Department: ______________________ Dept. Head Approval: ________

Location of Project: ______________________

Description of Project: ______________________

OFFICE USE ONLY
Work Done By: ______________________
Materials Used: ______________________

Date Completed: ______________________

FIGURE 31 - Work Request

Safety

Attention to safety is important since it communicates the message, "We care about you." A positive response to the following safety concerns will help communicate a "caring message."

1 Is the entrance to the school hazard free?
2 Do the entrance and exits provide clear lines of sight?
3 Is there proper fencing around the playground areas?
4 Are parking lots properly lighted?
5 Are rugs free of unsewn seams, worn holes, etc.?
6 Are wet floors marked with signs?
7 Have crosswalks and loading and unloading zones been properly marked or stripped?
8 Are speed limit and children at play signs posted on the property?
9 Are all ceiling tile intact?
10 Have abrasive strips been placed on ramps?
11 Are unusual changes in walking surfaces clearly high- lighted?
12 Is all playground equipment in good repair?

13 Are all electrical outlets covered?

14 Is there adequate ventilation in science labs?

15 Is all furniture in good repair?

16 Are stairways in good repair; i.e., hand railings, no frayed carpet, or cracked tiles?

17 Do shower facilities have adequate drains?

18 Are fire escape lamps lit?

19 Is an outside shut-off valve on the gas supply line provided?

20 Are spaces beneath stairs free of accumulations or storage of any materials?

21 Are fire evacuation plans posted in all classrooms?

22 Is there a master electrical cut-off switch conveniently located?

23 Do solid doors opening into the hallway have a viewing glass to prevent them from being opened into someone on the other side.

24 Are the science labs equipped with an approved fire blanket and eye wash kit?

25 Are corridors free of dead ends and obstructions?

26 Is first aid equipment available?

27 Are playground surfaces level and free of hazards? Fill in potholes and remove broken paving, loose stones and pebbles.

28 Is the campus free of bottles, cans and other trash? Formulate a "bottle patrol."

29 Are all fences in good repair - free of sharp edges and loose sections?

Learning Environment

The adequacy of the instructional environment influences the effectiveness of teaching, training and learning.

Research over the past 50 years has demonstrated the close relationship between learning and the visual, acoustical and thermal environments of the classroom. It has been demonstrated, school lighting and furniture designs are culprits in warping physical development and impeding educational progress in students.

It is true, learning can take place in almost any situation (classroom, playground, hallways, on the street, in the home, etc.); however, sustained instruction in poorly planned instructional space can result in adverse physiological reactions.

If you are operating your school in a facility built within the last 20 years for school use, you should experience few challenges with the visual, acoustical or thermal environments.

A good physical environment makes itself felt in many ways (Marks, et. al., 1971):

1 The student feels happier.

2 The student learns more quickly and has a feeling of pride in his school.

3 The teacher has more stamina and good morale.

4 The teacher is more patient and relaxed.

5 The need for discipline is lessened.

6 Vandalism may be negligible.

7 Custodial and maintenance costs diminish.

Does your school provide for a conducive learning environment that would draw students to your facilities? Consider the following.

Color

Does the color of the walls represent neutral tones, such as beige and tans, rather than reds, pinks, oranges and yellows which tend to promote stimulation and excitement?

Replace old grays and browns. Light colors will reflect in darker rooms and make small rooms look larger. Select paint with a low shine, preferably a latex enamel. This minimizes glare, and the walls are easier to clean.

Be careful not to use blues, greens, grays, lavenders, etc., where there is no natural lighting; these colors are repressive and often depressive.

Size and Variety

Are classrooms furnished differently, such as the kindergarten room versus the fourth grade room? It is important to provide for variety. Different sizes and shapes make a room more interesting. Cots, rugs, mats built-ins, benches, places for reading circles, adjustable desks, chairs, tables, etc. all add to making a classroom a special splace.

Paint ceilings white, because 80 percent reflection factor is needed to give pupils sufficient light.

Flexibility

Do furnishings provide for flexibility? Is it possible to arrange the furniture so orientation for full group activities can be toward a given presentation point?

Can the teacher and students' desk arrangements be made so there is easy movement between them? Maintain unobstructed access in all parts of the classroom. Maintain a minimum clear aisle of four feet for two-way traffic.

Noise

This may be the school located near a busy intersection or one having an older heating and ventilation system. Control classroom noise by the application of acoustical materials to the ceiling and walls, installation of carpet, lowering ceilings and increasing tack boards. If you have a large, noisy gym, multipurpose room, or corridor, you can reduce flutter and echoes by using sound boards and carpet. A carpeted hallway wall makes for a good display area. In carpeting walls, make sure that you purchase fire resistant, materials that meet building codes.

Lighting

Is lighting intensity within the 70 to 150 footcandles? Maximize the use of natural lighting. Many times interior rooms can access natural light by installing skylights. Light colored ceilings and walls increase lighting levels. Arrangement of classroom and office furniture can improve lighting.

It is important to check each room for the amount of glare from light sources to the student desks and chalk boards. You can reduce brightness of desk tops and wall surfaces by using a flat finish with a low reflection ratio. Inspect to assure lighting is uniformly distributed through the room with no area that has dark spots.

Equipment and Instructional Materials

Many Christian schools have been unsuccessful at recruiting and retaining students because of a lack of commitment to providing necessary equipment and instructional materials.

New or Used?

Schools have fallen in the trap mentioned by Deuink and Herbster (1986),

> "Schools do not want to give the impression . . . that their building committees raided a second-hand furniture store for equipment" (p. 80).

Antiquated and makeshift equipment leads students and parents to equate these to a poor-quality program.

On the other hand, don't overlook used equipment in good condition. With a little time invested and a few materials, used school desks secured from public schools can be refinished, and in many cases, are much better constructed than some of the newer furniture. It is not unusual to see school systems discard solid oak chairs in favor of new molded plastic.

Many times businesses in the process of up-grading office furniture are looking for a non-profit organization to receive equipment. When AMOCO upgraded its office furniture, it donated beautiful oak and walnut tables, chairs and office desks to Victory Christian School; this amounted to thousands of dollars in savings to the school.

Quality equipment and furnishings will pay for themselves through increased enrollment.

When Victory Christian School opened its high school, it was faced with the expense of adding typing to its high school course offerings. Confronted with the cost of typewriters, the question was, "Would the school ask parents for used typewriters they had at home or in their businesses? Would it look for some hand-me-downs from public school, or could the school believe God for new typewriters, the very best?

The school choose to believe God for the best and ordered 28 baby blue IBM electric student typewriters under a special educational payment plan. The idea was "the additional equipment would influence enrollment decisions." Once the typewriters were in place, every prospective student was given a tour of the new business lab. There is no doubt in anyone's mind, several students enrolled because of the new typewriters in the business lab.

The same was true when Victory added a $65,000 computer lab, and erected a $24,000 creative play center. We have learned to ask a simple question when faced with a decision of spending money to improve facilities and equipment, "Will this decision result in more students enrolling?" If the answer is positive, make the purchase and believe God for the necessary student increase.

Lockers

One item in the school often overlooked as contributing to recruiting and retaining students is lockers. As any administrator knows, school lockers are more than places to store books and gym shorts; they become the center for social gathering. Lockers are an important part of every school - but all too often students decide to make their mark on their lockers. After a few years, even a new school can have paint-worn lockers.

Even without vandalism, normal wear and tear can make lockers drab and dingy, handles get broken, numbers fall off, latching mechanisms don't work, locks no longer work. The way your lockers look affects the way your entire school looks. Replacing lockers may be a luxury your school cannot afford. Consider refurbishing them on site with Dura-Kote at a 25 to 40 percent saving over replacement costs (Contact Dura-Kote, Inc. P.O. Box 26309, Austin, TX 78755).

Furnishings and Equipment

How a school is furnished and the amount and kinds of equipment available influence enrollment decisions. Consider the following areas:

Visual Boards

Do the classrooms have approximately 16 to 24 linear feet of chalkboard space and 8 to 16 linear feet of bulletin board space? Chalkboards are a very important part of the instructional program. Investing in high-quality chalkboards will pay off in the long run.

When Victory opened its doors at 4400 South Sheridan, a decision had to be made to furnish the rooms with chalkboards. In getting rooms ready for students, a decision was made to purchase cheap, ready-to-ship chalkboards. By the end of the first year of operation, the chalkboards had seen their better day, and half of the boards had to be replaced or resurfaced.

Physical Education Facilities

Does the school have access to a gymnasium? If your school does not have adequate gym facilities, arrange gym time at the local YMCA. If no gyms are available, consider renovating an unoccupied warehouse. Does your school have any specialty rooms; e.g., music, art, cafeteria?

Furnishings

Is the working height of furniture and equipment at the proper height for the group of students who will be using them (K chairs = 10-11 inches; chairs for grades 1-3 = 10-13 inches; chairs for grades 4-6 = 12-16 inches: grades 7-12 chairs would range from 14-18 inches)?

Instructional Equipment

Is classroom instructional equipment adequate, for example, recorders, projectors, maps, globes, etc.?

Finally, allow teachers to be involved in the selection of classroom equipment since they are directly affected by the furnishings and equipment.

Maximize Use of School Facilities

The key word here is flexibility. The efficiency of the school plant utilization depends to a large degree upon the way in which various rooms can be used during all hours of the day.

Full Utilization

Any school not fully utilizing its facilities is running the risk of being criticized for not being good stewards of God's resources. Developing a room usage chart of all available classroom space will provide a bird'seye view of rooms that are in use and empty rooms for each period of the day.

Inspection of a room usage chart (See Figure 32) should illustrate potentialities, such as multipurpose rooms, furnishing of

The following classroom diagram illustrates the correct furniture arrangement. It is the user's responsibility to arrange the room exactly as illustrated. Please indicate which days you will be using the classroom by placing a X in the proper box. Indicate a.m. or p.m. usage.

Dates	VCS	Rangers	Missionettes	Sunday School
Mon a.m. p.m.				
Tue a.m. p.m.				
Wed a.m. p.m.				
Thu a.m p.m.				
Fri a.m. p.m.				
Sat a.m. p.m.				
Sun a.m. p.m.				

F

F

F

General Rules:

1. All chalkboards erased after use.
2. All paper picked up and placed in trash containers.
3. Doors shut, lights off when leaving.
4. Person in charge of room use is responsible for all wall arrangements and property.

FIGURE 32 - Room Usage

classrooms for dual use and use of specialized areas for more than one purpose. For example, Victory Christian School's kindergarten classrooms are used on Wednesday night for children's program, while the high school classrooms become a room for students in Victory Bible Institute and Victory World Missions Training School.

By constructing a "building utilization chart," the degree of utilization can be determined. The chart lists the rooms by number and kind and gives the following data:

1 Number of students in each room.

2 Daily capacity of each room based on the average of 25 square feet per student.
3 Daily utilization of each room.
4 Percentage of utilization determined by dividing item 3 by item 2 (above for each room).
5 Total percentage of utilization for entire building is determined by dividing room percentages.

Open Your Building to the Public

Making your facility available for special events provides additional exposure to the community. What if those who enter your building are attracted to Christian education by what they see and feel? But you may say, "You can lead a horse to the water, but you can't make him drink." What if you ran your horse around the pasture a few times first until he got thirsty? Do you think he would take a drink? Allowing groups to have access to your building, viewing your attractive hallways, creative bulletin boards, visual displays of student work and attractive classrooms, may not lead some to enroll, but it will provide a strong impression for the Holy Spirit to use for enrollment success.

The first time we entered Holland Hall, a private college preparatory school, during a book fair, we were extremely impressed with the creative use of the building and variety of furnishings. In the summer when our son was looking for a SAT review course, we remembered what we had seen at Holland Hall and enrolled him in their course.

Special Events

The following is a list of special events to use in attracting prospects to your school.

1. Conduct a SAT and ACT preparatory course.
2. Place community voting machines.
3. Sponsor a Christian Businessmen's Fair.
4. Endorse a Christian Home Show.
5. Sponsor concerts, dramas, etc.
6. Offer the building as a civil defense center.
7. Conduct a community job fair.
8. Sponsor a college fair.

9. Hold a city-wide spelling bee, academic bowl, etc.
10. Do a wills and estate planning seminar.
11. Conduct an arts and crafts fair.
12. Hold a fashion show.
13. Sponsor a health fair.
14. Conduct a financial planning workshop.
15. Offer your building for an area science fair.

Many organizations are reluctant to offer their facilities because of the additional commitment of time and energy, the need to establish facility usage policies, application procedures, secuity, equitable rates and insurance. However, the positive benefits of exposing your school to the community are worth it.

Planning Tips

Plan the event carefully and keep it to a size that you can manage. It is better to start small and achieve first-class success than to plan too large and end up with a marginal success that leaves doubt as to whether it should have been attempted the first time - or ever again.

Provide information to the media as to the purpose of the event and sponsorship. Avoid giving the impression that you are more interested in the media coverage than the event being sponsored (Yarrington, 1983). This may be done in the name attached to the event, in a printed program, in announcements, introductory remarks, signs, or many other ways.

Do a quality job on the event, keeping in mind the public will make its judgment on the quality of the event.

Believe God for Creative Ways to Meet Facility Needs

When Victory Christian School first opened its doors in 1979, 226 students enrolled in grades K4-6th. The following year, grades 7-12 were added and enrollment doubled to 446. Every corner, hallway and closet were in use. Not only had the school grown, but the church had exploded; six services were being held on Sundays in order to accommodate the people.

It was obvious something had to be done. Plans were made to build a new church and school on the same location. However, the city planning commission rejected the proposal. Pastor Billy

Joe Daugherty, along with the staff, began to speak out and believe "for a building they had not built and parking lots they had not paved." In a matter of months, God opened up the opportunity to purchase a used auto dealership with 60,000 square feet.

Look Not at Things as They Are, But as They Will Be

We still remember the day in April, walking through the building and seeing row after of row of auto hoists. It took a lot of faith to see beyond the physical appearance of the auto mart. God performed a miracle, and the building was renovated to accommodate classrooms, a sanctuary and church and school offices by fall.

We did not have room for physical education facilities so students were transported to a nearby YMCA and indoor soccer arena. The front showcase rooms were converted into a library, while the sales offices became computer cubicles. Part of the parking lot was covered with dirt and sod to make room for a soccer field and recess area.

Enrollment climbed to 585 students the first year and reached its maximum of 680 students in two years. By this time the church had outgrown the sanctuary.

Once again, God spoke to Pastor. This time it was to offer the property for sale. He was quickened that the property would sell in mid-year, knowing an alternative location would be necessary if the school was to continue. Only one site, a former junior high school with 94,000 square feet, was available that would meet the needs of the ministry. On six separate occasions, an offer to lease Thoreau Junior High School was presented to the board of education, and on six different occasions, the offer was refused.

Keep on Knocking Until The Door Opens

The week school started, Pastor was impressed in his spirit to approach the school board one final time, and to everyone's utter amazement, the school board approved the lease.

On Thursday and Friday of the first week of school the students, staff, members and friends of Victory Christian School, packed and moved the entire school to Thoreau Junior High School and the school was ready for classes on Monday.

The next fall, enrollment increased to 780 students. A waiting list began to develop. No one likes to wait. As we mentioned previously, a waiting list, unless carefully managed, produces negative effects upon enrollment.

With 16 students already on the waiting list and the start of school still two months away, a decision was made to look for portable classrooms as an alternative. Visits were made to several public schools where portable buildings were in use. A double classroom unit was purchased for $3,000. Moving, renovations and bringing the building to city code standards cost an additional $13,000.

The commitment to add two more classrooms resulted in the 16 students on the waiting list being enrolled; once the word was out that Victory had more space, enrollment increased to 835 students. This resulted in $90,000 additional income - more than enough to pay for the portable classrooms, additional teachers and equipment. In addition, when the school moved to its new site, the portable building was sold.

Through the help of God, the ministry was able to purchase land and build a beautiful 200,000 square feet church and school building debt free just across the street from Oral Roberts University Campus.

God has performed miracle after miracle, enabling His work to go forward. We believe God can activate your faith as he did Pastor Billy Joe Daugherty's, staff, and members and friends ofVictory Christian Center; you will have the exact school site, or classroms, at the right time to meet the needs of your students.

Never underestimate the influence of the physical condition and general appearance of the school facilities on student recruitment and retention.

9

Provide the Best Education for the Lowest Possible Cost

What if anyone who wanted to come to your school could do so free of charge? How many would come? If this were the case, you would no longer have a challenge recruiting students; you would have a challenge of, "How to deal with a waiting list." And, if your school provides quality programs, there would be no challenge retaining students.

The number one concern of parents seeking to enroll their children in a Christian school is finances. In fact, finances are the major concern expressed by administrators in keeping their schools open.

We estimate upwards of 75 percent of the families enrolled in Christian schools experience financial sacrifice in keeping their child in school. For many families, enrolling is a step of faith followed by believing God for each month's tuition. Some find it necessary to obtain a second or third job, while others rearrange their financial priorities.

Generating the income to pay for the educational programs requires schools to rely on tuition and fees. Yet, each time tuition and fees are increased, a private Christian school education becomes further and further out of reach of many families. In addition to funds coming from tuition and fees, Christian schools obtain income from other funding sources, such as fund-raising campaigns, grants, etc. However, when a school relies on more than 20 percent of income from outside sources, it is deemed by many Christian educators to be "at risk." That is, "What would happen if these outside funding sources were suddenly cut off?"

If increasing tuition is not feasible and outside financial sources are limited, schools have two other choices: increase enrollment or reduce expenses. However, if expenses are reduced too drastically, over time, the quality of programs will be affected and eventually, student enrollment declines. The solution is to provide the best educational program at the lowest possible cost.

Up to this point, we have presented strategies for improving a school's education program in order to attract more students. This chapter provides strategies for adjusting spending and income plans, thus making a private Christian school education more affordable.

Offer Creative Tuition Plans

Those schools operating on a full-cost tuition plan should consider an adjusted tuition cost plan. This would allow more families to enroll their children.

Percent Reduction

These plans may take several forms. Rather than charging parents the full tuition cost, a specified percentage of the total cost will be raised through various fund raising projects. The remaining 90 percent of the projected costs are divided by the number of students expected. For example: $50,000 Operational Costs, -$5,000 for fund-raising, leaves $45,000. This divided by 40 students = $1,125 per student.

Multiple Member Discount

Another adjusted cost tuition plan provides a multiple family member discount whereby the per pupil tuition cost decreases by a certain percentage or fixed amount for each additional family member. Caution must be exercised in accurately projecting the expected number of first, second, third, or fourth children. Calculating an adjusted tuition level using a percentage plan is very easy. Deuink (1985) provides the following formula: $F_1B + F_2\ (\%B) + F_3\ (\%B) = OC$, where F_1 equals the number of students from one child families, F_2 represents the number of students from two children families, F_3 stands for the number of children enrolled from families with three children, %B represents the percentage of base tuition established and OC depicts the schools operational costs (See Table 4).

TABLE 4 - Multiple Member Discount

Operation Cost (OC) = $50,000				
# of Children	Family Member	% of Base	Tuition Rate	Tuition Rounded
25	F1	100	$1312	$1315
13	F2	90	$1181	$1180
2	F3	70	$919	$920
Formula $F_1B + F_2(5\%) + F_3(\%B) = OC$				

Tuition Range Adjustment

A third adjusted tuition plan provides a real dollar reduction in tuition based on the earning ability of parents rather than the number of members in the family. This is accomplished by identifying various ranges of gross family income and then establishing corresponding tuition rates for families with one child, two children, etc. (See Table 5).

This plan is best instituted following the first year of operation when you have had an opportunity to establish the income ranges of your school families. Include on your application a place where parents can identify their particular range of income. Parents who want to take advantage of the adjusted tuition plan will need to

TABLE 5 - Tuition Range Adjustment

Range	% Reduction For 1-2 Children	% Reduction for 3-4 Children	% Reduction for 5+ Children
$20,000+	0	0	0
15,000-19,999	1	2	3
12,000-14,999	2	3	4
9,000-11,999	5	6	10
Below 9,000	10	15	20

provide copies of their previous year's income taxes. This will reduce the major challenge of verifying family incomes.

Tuition Gift Certificate

Parents can purchase tuition gift certificates at 1/100th of a full year's tuition at the time of purchase. The school insures the relative value of the unit remains intact as tuition increases. Parents can trade in the certificates, thereby gaining an edge against inflation.

Money collected from the gift certificates is invested by the school in order to gain interest. Everyone wins when the interest gained in greater than the percent of tuition increase. No refunds are provided on investments, but the school can allow the purchaser to redesignate the certificate to another student if the first designated student does not enroll or re-enroll.

Tuition Assistance Programs

Since it may not be possible for some parents to send their children to a Christian school even when special tuition plans are available, consideration should be given to a tuition assistance or scholarship program. The following guidelines are suggested:

1 **Establish assistance or scholarship funds as a restricted account.** This will provide a greater accountability of funds as well as assuring donors' contributions will go to a specific project.

2 **Develop a special brochure**. Use this for people who are interested in contributing to the fund. Indicate all contributions to a general scholarship fund are tax deductible, while monies given to a particular student are not deductible.

3 **Provide written guidelines**. Outline the conditions for qualification as well as the steps to follow in making application. For example, consider providing tuition assistance to qualifying widows, missionaries, ministers, truly fatherless and single parents.

4 **Formalize the application process**. The formal application should ask for basic demographic information, listing of joint income, listing of assets-savings, cash, checking account, property, insurance, stocks, etc., major financial setbacks, a

statement as to why they should be considered for assistance, a minimum amount requested, and a statement from the parent as to the importance of a Christian education (See Appendix K for a sample of a Tuition Assistance Application).

5 **Notify parents of the receipt of the application.** We recommend returning an incomplete application to parents for completion before it can be reviewed.

6 **Use cut-off dates.** Print on the application the cut-off date for receiving applications. We recommend all applications be in no later than 14 days before school commences.

7 **Appoint a tuition assistance review board.** This board should consist of no less than three members. Their responsibilities include: reviewing each application; making awards based on priority of need; and communicating awards in writing to parents or guardian.

Work Study Programs

We caution schools who have work study programs where parents exchange work (e.g., secretarial, custodial) for tuition. In the sight of IRS, this is interpreted as taxable income and should be subject to income tax. If a parent's taxes are audited, the school increases its risk of being audited. To help parents avoid the unreported income challenge, we recommend the following:

1 Establish a certain number of jobs to be considered as work study.

2 Write a job description for each position.

3 Hire the parent and pay them by check.

4 Have the parent sign the check back over to the school to be applied to their tuition, or better yet, provide for a payroll deduction in the amount of the check.

The only challenge to this plan is the school must consider the parent an employee and is therefore responsible for withholding taxes, paying social security (unless considered self-employed) and workers compensation. As an employee, they may also meet the qualifications to receive employee benefits.

Tuition Credit

Provide a tuition reduction incentive for families who are solely responsible for the enrollment of a new family. Any parent or student may earn credit towards their tuition for each new student referred to and accepted by the school. The amount of credit allowed can be established on a monthly allowance: e.g., $10 per month for each month the new student attends up to a maximum of nine months. In other words, a person could earn a total of $90 per referred student in any one school year. You may or may not want to establish a limit to the number of referrals accepted.

To reduce the amount of paperwork, you might award the total amount of $90 for every new student enrolled provided the student remains in school for at least two months. Parents can be motivated even further by identifying new students as anyone who has not attended school for at least one year and is not a member of the immediate family. This helps in re-enrolling former students (See Appendix L).

Evaluate Your Fee Structure

Most schools require various fees. The way in which these fees are established and communicated to parents will influence enrollment decisions.

Enrollment Fees

Most schools charge an enrollment fee which is generally non-refundable and covers the cost of promotional packets, enrollment forms, entrance testing, supplies, etc. This fee is set high enough so parents will give careful thought to enrollment, yet not too high as to discourage enrollment. This fee may range in the neighborhood of $50 to $150.

Although a school may elect to charge a re-enrollment fee each year, consider charging a one-time enrollment fee at the time of initial enrollment and not charging a re-enrollment fee as long as the student remains a continuous student at the school.

Whatever enrollment fee system you develop, do not keep changing it from year to year. If enrolling requires a "one time" fee, do not go back on your word and add a re-enrollment fee the following year; it would be better to increase tuition.

Book Fees

There are two major textbook fee plans: 1) student purchase plan, and 2) student rental plan. Under a purchase plan, the school purchases books from vendors; parents then purchase the books at retail prices. The books are theirs to keep, and may be resold back to the school at the end of the school term, or sold to other parents during a book exchange day.

A rental plan places the responsibility for the care of books on both the student and the school. Parents are charged a rental fee pro-rated on the life of the book. Workbooks are rated at full cost for a year and given to students to keep at the end of the school year. Paperback books are pro-rated over a two-year period. Hardback books are pro-rated over three years.

Inventory logs are kept by each teacher including the number of the book and its condition. Other than the workbooks, all other books are collected at the end of the school year. Students with damaged books beyond normal usage are charged a book repair fee. Students who lose books are required to pay the remaining portion to replace the book.

There are two advantages of this plan. First of all, as soon as books are collected at the end of the year, you know exactly how many new books are to be purchased for the new school year. Secondly, you can reduce the cost to the parent by pro-rating the replacement costs over a three- to five-year period.

If a rental fee is used, establish it as an average rental fee per school division, such as kindergarten, grades 1-3, grades 4-6, grades 7-8 and grades 9-12. This keeps the number of different fees to a minimum, eases accounting procedures and gives the impression to parents, "We are getting a good deal." For example, given a fee of $140, students in grades 7-12 receive all of their books (rented), all labs paid, a student ID card, a copy of the school yearbook and accident insurance.

This initial fee might seem high at first, but parents appreciate paying for everything at once, rather than being assessed a variety of fees. A school might consider a special incentive for early enrollment during a specified period of time by waving this fee.

Purchasing hardcover books, especially when you utilize a rental system, will extend the replacement time, thereby reducing the per student rental cost. Ensure students cover all books to be returned; consider purchasing standardized school covers with your school logo and other information (calendar, code of conduct, policies, etc.) on one side of the cover.

Athletic Participation Fees

Many Christian schools require athletic fees to be paid to help offset athletic programs. The general guideline for establishing fees should be directly related to the cost of the program. For example, all students participating in a sport pay a $15 fee per sport at the elementary level, not to exceed a total of $30. At the junior and senior high school levels, this fee is set at around $25 per sport with a maximum for any one student of $50. To help offset the cost for families, have a maximum of $100 for a single family.

Some schools charge a student activity fee ($5-$10). Consideration might be given to creating a family activity fee ($20-$30) which allows everyone from the immediate family to participate in sporting events without having to pay at the gate. All they need to do is show their activity card. You may also consider including a student activity card as part of the sports enrollment fee.

Other Fees

Some schools require students to pay for special programs such as private music lessons, drivers education, science labs, home economics labs, etc. The rationale for this plan is, "Since not all students participate in all of these programs, only those students who are involved should pay." Usually, high school students are the ones who end up paying additional fees.

The main drawback is upper-level students paying more fees. When you add to these fees, money for athletics, junior/senior banquet, class rings, senior pictures, graduation announcements, to name a few, the cost rapidly rises. Spreading fees out over all grades lessens the financial load for upper-level students. Recalculate all of these additional fees as a single fee payment.

Collect Tuition

Since the main portion of your school's income will come from tuition, it is important you establish an effective collection system. Failure to pay tuition places an unnecessary financial load on all parents. There are five main approaches to tuition collection.

Payment by Cash or Check

Once the tuition has been calculated, parents may elect to pay with cash or check on a monthly basis. Tuition is usually due on the first of the month. A grace period of five days may be given before a late payment fee is charged. You may send parents monthly statements of their account, or use a coupon book approach similar to those used to repay bank auto loans. In addition to a monthly payment plan, we recommend a discount for tuition paid by the year (6-10 percent) or by the semester (2-5 percent). Monies collected on semester or yearly payment plans provide available cash for "start up" expenditures.

The major challenge with this plan is the tendency for some families to write checks that bounce because of insufficient funds. Unless you have a very efficient deposit system, it may take two weeks before notification is received of the insufficient funds checks. By the time you notify parents of the insufficient funds, and ask them to write a new check, or send through the old insufficient funds check, two to three additional weeks may have passed. Even when a second check is submitted, you have no assurance sufficient funds are in the account unless you call the bank. All of this adds to the uncertainty of just how much cash you have to operate for school. Since most Christian schools operate on a tight budget, it takes all families paying their tuition on time in order for the educational plan to continue as scheduled. After the second IFS check, we recommend requiring parents to pay in cash, by money order, or cashier's check.

Automatic Payment

Some schools have instituted an automatic tuition collection system whereby parents authorize the school to deduct from their savings or checking account the monthly tuition (See Figure 33). An electronic transfer is made from the parent's bank to the school's account on a specified day each month.

Automatic Payment Authorization

I wish to use Victory Christian School's automatic bank authorization card. I have read the terms and conditions, and I understand and agree to them.

Name of Student(s) - Please Print

Street City State Zip

Name of Parent or Guardian (Please Print)Phone (Home)(Work)

Financial Institution

Checking Account Number - Attach a Deposit Slip or Voided Check with Account No.

I authorize $___________ to be charged to my account on or after the 9th of each month.

Signature of Individual Whose Checking Acct. Will Be Charged

Date____________________

FIGURE 33 - Automatic Payment Authorization

The advantage for the school is in knowing two days following the bank draft how much money has been transferred into the school's account, as well as which parent accounts have insufficient funds. The bank assesses a $15 insufficient funds charge to each parent whose account had insufficient funds. The school in turn charges a $10 insufficient funds fee. These IFS fees are strong encouragements for parents to have sufficient funds in their account at the time the automatic draft takes place.

Parents with IFS notices can be called immediately and asked to bring in cash, traveler's check, money order, or cashier's check to apply toward the insufficient funds draft.

Educational Loan

Another technique for collecting tuition involves arranging with a local lending institution for parents to obtain an educational loan. Parents secure a loan from the lending institution as the school being the co-signature on the bank note.

The lending institution transfers the loan dollars into the school's account. The main advantage is the school has its operating funds up front at the beginning of the school term and the lending institution pays the school interest on unused monies. Parents in turn deal directly with the bank rather than the school on nine- to twelve-month payment plans.

The main disadvantage is the school assumes the parents indebtedness if they withdraw from school. Also, the parents are charged interest on the loan, and it is an encouragement toward indebtedness. This may present a challenge for those schools sponsored by a church which encourages its members to be debt free.

Credit Cards

With the wide availability of credit cards, it would stand to reason this would be a very attractive option for Christian schools.

The disadvantage to the school is the percentage charged for participation with the credit card agency. The school must also buy, rent, or lease card machines, maintain valid lists and fill out detailed records in order to be paid.

Furthermore, it encourages indebtedness and results in parents paying high interest rates on the unpaid charge account balance.

Trust Funds

Generally, we think of trust funds only for college education. However, it is possible to establish a trust fund for Christian schooling grades K-12. Contact your accountant for more information on an educational trust.

Improve Collections

Regardless of the plan your school chooses to collect tuition, the following recommendations will improve your collection rate:

Evaluate the Parent's Ability to Pay

As part of your application process, ask the parent to identify the family income range prior to taxes. The higher the income level, the greater the probability of the family to pay tuition.

Check to see the type of job each parent has. Check to see if they have an outstanding balance at any other Christian school

(See Figure 34). If there are questions about the parent's ability to pay, conduct a credit check.

Clarification of Accounts
(One Per Family)

It is our commitment as a school to enroll only those families who do not have outstanding accounts at another Christian school. If you do have an outstanding balance, you will need to make arrangements to clear this balance before your child(ren) can attend class.

1. I testify that I have no outstanding balances with any other Christian school.

Signature of parent (guardian) Date

2. I have an outstanding account with ______________________
(Name of School)

3. Satisfactory arrangements have been made with the school to clear this balance.

____
Signature of parent (guardian) Date

Names of children enrolled and grades (Please Print)

____
____
____
____
____

FIGURE 34 - Clarification of Accounts

Obtain Commitment in Writing

The logical consequence of failure to meet a tuition obligation would be to withdraw the children from school. We do an injustice to parents when we allow delinquent accounts to continue to accumulate to a point where what was once a few hundred dollars becomes thousands: the small molehill becomes a mountain. Furthermore, it is not right for some parents to go through extreme sacrifice and self-denial to keep their accounts current, while others fall further and further behind, yet keep their children in school (See Figure 35).

Payment Agreement

1. I understand grade cards and official transcripts will not be released until my account in paid in full - to include any and all handling fees.

2. I agree that my account must be current at the end of each grading period in order for my child(ren) to be allowed to remain in school the next grading period.

3. I agree that any time there are insufficient funds to pay the monthly automatic bank draft or a check payment, I will pay VCS a $20 handling fee in addition to any fees my bank may charge for handling such a draft or check, and that I will pay both the missed payment and $20 fee no later than the ninth (9th) of the next month.

4. I agree that any time I find it necessary to not have an automatic bank draft payment withheld from my account, I will notify the school business office not later than five (5) working days prior to the ninth of the month, and that I will pay VCS a $20 handling fee for having the draft temporarily canceled.

5. I agree that if I withdraw my child(ren) officially or unofficially, before the end of the school year, I will have added to my account and will pay any book fees which I was not charged due to re-enrolling my chid(ren) before the March 31st deadline.

6. All withdrawals after the 1st of the month will be charged the entire month's tuition.

7. Any withdrawals prior to the end of the school year will be assessed the full book costs.

____

Father/Guardian Date

____

Mother/Guardian Date

FIGURE 35 - Payment Agreement

Provide Immediate Follow-up on Accounts

First of all, mail statements. Use a special designed statement form rather than the regular school stationary. Use special type to direct attention to key information; e.g. outstanding balance or withdrawal pending. Use the words, "please pay" instead of "amount due" as request for action. Accounts that become delinquent receive a letter followed by a personal phone call.

Dun and Bradstreet (1985) provide the following tips in making collection phone calls.

1. Call plan sheet. Develop a pre-call plan sheet (outstanding balance, previous communications).

2. Determine a payment plan. The purpose of the phone call is to collect the full amount owed. Since this will most likely not be possible in all cases, have a payment plan in mind. Your payment plan will depend on amount owed, parent's circumstances and your own school policies. You will have a better chance of collection if your plan can be adjusted to meet the parent's needs.

3. Prepare a good opening statement. First, identify yourself. "Mr. Smith, I am the administrator for Victory Christian School. Our business office referred your account to my attention. It appears there is some discrepancy concerning when payment would be made on your tuition. May I take a few moments of your time to resolve it?"

4. Be prepared to deal with standard excuses. Make a list of the common excuses you hear, take each one and write down the information you believe you most want to know when someone offers the excuse. If someone says "I lost my job," you might ask: "How long have you been unemployed?" "When do you expect to be back to work?" "How are you handling bills that just can't wait until you go back to work?" "Which of your bills are you keeping up to date?"

5. Prepare a lead-in to your payment plan. An effective lead-in to your payment plan allows the parent to know your concern in helping them bring their tuition account up to date. An example: "We want to help you bring your tuition up to current status as soon as possible. Based on the information you have given me, how does this sound. . . ."

6. Establish the benefits of your payment plan. Depending upon your policies, you can speak of continued enrollment and their children's uninterrupted educational program; there are no additional costs, late payment fees, interest, or the like.

Use a Confirmation Letter

Confirm phone conversations and arrangements to pay past-due tuition with a confirmation letter.

Put the letter in the mail as soon as possible, preferably no later than the following day. The letter does two things: it shows how concerned you are about the past-due tuition and that you are holding true to the arrangements you have made with the parent; it eradicates any excuse they might later provide.

Adjust Income Projections

Regardless of how hard you try, there will always be those parents who fall behind in tuition and may end up withdrawing before you are able to collect past-due tuition. Once withdrawal takes place, the chances of collecting tuition are greatly diminished.

The best way to prepare for this short fall is to adjust your original budget. Victory Christian School projects a 95 percent collection rate. Further adjustments are made following the first week of operation.

Withhold Records and Prohibit Re-enrollment

Establish a policy of withholding report cards and sending out official transcripts for students whose accounts are past due.

Require parents with outstanding accounts from the previous year to have their account cleared in order to re-enroll for the new school term.

Request a Budget

Require families who establish a history of payment challenges to develop and submit a family budget. Establish an appointment to review their budget and provide financial counseling where needed. Consider adding a financial management concepts class to your Sunday school program or on Saturday mornings in the school. Require all parents with outstanding accounts to attend a financial management seminar held on a Friday night and Saturday morning. (See Larry Burkett's, *Your Finances in Changing Times*, 1982).

Train Your Parents in "Seed Faith" Principles

Oral Roberts, when asked how he had accomplished the things that he had in his ministry, answered, "By living and practicing three key principles of Seed Faith."

1. **God is your source**. The Bible says "**But my God shall supply all your need according to his riches in glory by Christ**

Jesus" (Philippians 4:19). God is the parent's and school's source of financial supply.

2. **Give and it shall be given to you.** Jesus said "**Give, and it shall be given unto you; good measure, pressed down, and shaken together, and running over, shall men give into your bosom. For with the same measure that ye mete withal it shall be measured to you again**" (Luke 6:38).

Oral Roberts puts it this way: "Whatever you give becomes a seed that you plant for God to multiply back. But you initiate the action. You give first. You continually look for ways to give your love, your talent, your time and earnings - anything that represents you (and we add, your school). You give until it becomes a part of you. . .and God multiplies the seed sown back to you in the form of your personal need" (Roberts, 1982).

3. **Expect a miracle.** Expect God to perform a financial miracle. As you do your part in planting seeds and releasing your faith for the harvest, God will provide the miracle. Last year, Victory Christian School set aside $50,000 of its tuition income to be used as tuition assistance for needy families, mainly children of widows, missionaries and the truly fatherless.

Clarify Your Faith in God's Provision

Make this declaration of faith:

Father, I thank You that the hand of the devourer is rebuked over the finances of the families in this school. The devil's hold over their finances is broken in Jesus' Name. Spirit of poverty and lack, you are bound in the Name of Jesus. We speak the release of blessings to every household. Let a bountiful harvest come from all the seeds that have been planted.

Father, I thank You that the families in our school meet their tuition payments on time and that they have enough to give unto every good work. Father, our families hearken unto the voice of the Lord their God, and all the blessings you have for them shall come on them and overtake them.

Collection Agencies

Over the past few years, there has been a strong, steady increase in the use of collection agencies as a means of collecting tuition. The thought behind the use of an outside agency is most Christian schools are poor bill collectors. Rather than pressing a parent for tuition to be paid on time, the school extends mercy. Although mercy is a positive trait, mercy will not pay the bills.

Invariably, schools continue to allow accounts to go delinquent to a point where it jeopardizes the education welfare of the school. In some cases, when the school does make a decision to withdraw children because of past-due tuition, the school risks the loss of a past-due account amounting to thousands of dollars.

If you decide to use a collection agency, view the collection agency as an extension of your school. As such, draw up specific guidelines identifying what type of performance you expect, as well as the nature and tone of the collection activities. Familiarize yourself with the agency's past record and obtain references. All it takes is one disgruntled parent frustrated over an agency's attempt to collect $500 of past-due tuition, resulting in several families withdrawing their children from school.

Supplement Tuition and Fee Income with Fund-raising

Fund-raising in a necessary activity of most Christian schools. Consider the following eight elements for effective fund-raising projects:

1. Develop a plan with realistic goals.
2. Select the fund-raising project(s) that will help achieve your goal.
3. Identify who is to be involved.
4. Organize your materials. Forms are essential to keep accurate and efficient records.
5. Communicate the need to staff, students and parents. Call attention to the cause, give goals and motivate toward action.
6. Launch the project and set up a timetable of events.
7. Run the project for a two week maximum time period.
8. Close and evaluate the program.

Fund-raising should be limited to no more than 20 percent of the operating budget. In addition, limit fund-raising to no more than four major schoolwide events per year. Staying within these recommendations will avoid fund-raising overload and close the door to negative opinion about the financial stability of the school.

One of the biggest drawbacks to fund-raising is the amount of teacher and instructional time that is consumed by administrative activities. Consider enlisting parent volunteers or hiring a person to oversee these activities.

Selling Services and Sales

Table 6 presents some effective fund-raising suggestions:

TABLE 6 - Fund-raising Ideas

SELLING SERVICES	SALES
Catering	Bazaars
Rental	Auctions
Lawn Cutting	Garage
Babysitting	Next to New Shop
Odd Jobs	Fun Fair
Car Wash	Art Show
Windows Washed	Crafts
Workshops	Flowers
Camps	Baskets
Gift Wrapping	Jewelry
Toy Repair	Smoked Turkeys and Ham
Day Nursery	World's Finest Candy
Concerts	Cookbooks
Dog and Cat Sitting	Pizza
Puppet Theater	T-Shirts
Christmas Trees	Cheese and Sausage

Continuing Sources

The following fund-raising events, once established, can be held each year: Magazine sales and renewals, labels and coupons, jog-a-thon and other thons. (This is a good activity to use for physical education equipment, creative play center, etc.) A raffle and lottery should not be considered as a fund-raiser regardless of the cause.

Extended school programs, before and after school, have a tremendous potential for extra income. Parents pay up to $26 per week, which includes two hours before school starts and after school hours until 6 p.m. In the morning, students can choose any number of activities, including reading. In the afternoon, offer courses in computers, foreign language, time for homework and opportunities for play (See Appendix M).

Network Marketing

Network marketing strategies hold tremendous potential for fund-raising income. Network marketing will account for over $40 billion in sales in 1991. It is estimated 50 percent of the products and services sold in the 90's will be through network marketing. Presently, three out of every four persons have purchased goods or services through network marketing. Many of the Fortune 500 companies recognize the value of network marketing.

Christian schools have a tremendous opportunity to cash in on the fastest growing concept of the 90's. Network marketing has a very low risk and a tremendous potential for high return on investment of finances and time. Money that normally goes to the middle man would come to the school. For more information on network marketing, contact the authors.

Fund-raising Schedules

In ministries where groups from the ministry and those from the school are doing fund raising, consider assigning one person to the task of reviewing and approving all fund-raising requests (See Figure 36). All approved activities should be placed on a master calendar to avoid overlap.

Groups should be encouraged to take fund-raising activities to different clientele each time rather than "hitting up" the same

Fund-raising Request

Group : ______

Number in group: ______

Sponsor: ______

Purpose of this event: ______

Target population to be approached: ______

Goal (How much $): ______

Date of fund-raiser: ______

Description of fund-raising activities: ______

______

______

Start-up costs: ______

Projected profit: ______

FIGURE 36 - Fund-raising Request

group every time. Also, for those families who do not participate in fund-raising events, consideration should be given to assessing these families the full cost of tuition.

Consider Other Proven Income Strategies

Some Christian schools have been successful in securing funds and equipment through the following:

1 **Donations**. Donations of money and gifts of equipment from individuals or organizations. The Bible says we have not because we ask not. If we ask and seek, we will find. The same holds true in fund-raising.

2 **Grants and bequests from foundations**. The school generally invests the initial gift and uses interest or profits from investments for the school's general fund.

3 **Partnerships**. Adopt-a-School program and other partnership with business and industry. Begin with your present vendor list.

4 **Active investment programs**. This is used for cash holdings generated from tuition paid by semester or year and earns interest on money not immediately needed.

5 **Booster clubs and parent-teacher organizations**.

6 **Living gifts**. These include: life insurance; real estate; personal property; stocks and bonds. (For a complete discussion of these gifts, see *Financing Christian Schools* by Philip Elve.)

7 **Founders clubs**. Establish clubs for individuals, organizations, corporations, or foundations donating $500 to $1,000 to start the new school or school year. Other clubs can be formed such as the 5:15:5 Club, where there are 500 people pledging $15 per month for five years.

8 **Letter campaigns**. This techniques should be used for a specific need and done in an expert fashion, short and to the point.

9 **Sales for equipment programs**. Major vendors, such as Pepsi, will help sponsor school equipment when the school signs up as an exclusive product school. Basketball equipment, score boards, etc. are items funded using this method.

10 **Support-A-Winner**. Individuals and churches are given an opportunity to adopt a student by helping with the Christian school costs (See Appendix N).

11 **Memorials**. Living memorials, or gifts given in memory of another person. Memorial gifts are tax deductible for the giver.

12 **Matching gifts**. Many companies will match gifts given by an employee to an educational institution. Have parents check with their employers to see if a gift matching program is available.

13 **Sustaining membership**. Special groups such as newly married couples with a new child, are contacted and asked to become a sustaining member of the school. They are committed to praying for the school, devoting time and talents and planting financial seeds into the school ministry.

14 **Faith promise dinners**. This fund-raiser yields immediate cash flow, numerous small donors and gives a pool of human resources for future volunteer projects.

15 **Radio day**. Obtain permission from your area Christian radio station to have your school participate in selling radio spots to vendors in the community to sponsor a day of programming by the students. The students make up ads and DJ the entire program.

16 **Alumni**. Don't overlook the valuable resources in the hands of school alumni.

17 **Capital drive**. This activity is best for raising large sums of money. Contact Christian schools or churches who have had successful capital drive campaigns, and secure the assistance of professionals who specialize in capital programs.

18 **Sales tax rebate**. Check with your city government. Some cities provide a sales tax rebate. Write a letter to your parents encouraging them to donate their sales tax rebates to be used to purchase equipment for the school.

Evaluate Federal and State Funding Opportunities

Although there is state and federal money available to be used by private schools, be cautious of any programs leading to compromise of the philosophy of your school: opening your records to audit; requiring employment of certain groups of individuals; e.g. homosexuals.

When possible, it is best to accept no federal money. However, if you do accept federal or state money, do not use these funds for basic programs; if you should decide to stop accepting federal or state funds, your basic program will not be affected.

Reduce Operating Costs

Every Christian school can find ways of reducing expenses. All it takes is a little investigation. Consider the following list of possible cost-reducing measures.

Staffing

1 Make good use of volunteers, especially for non-instructional tasks.

2 Consider cooperative services with other Christian schools; e.g., data processing, pooling use of maintenance specialists, volume purchasing, etc.

3. Require administrators and counselors to serve as substitutes two days per year.
4. Employ temporary help for peak work loads rather than regular clerical help.
5. Employ a librarian as part of consortium of Christian schools.
6. Use in-house staff for teacher development rather than consultants.
7. Offer a reward to employees for ideas that save more than $500 per year.

Financial Management

1. Shop around for the best price.
2. Defer capital spending until replacement services are established.
3. Place spending priorities on essential programs.
4. Reduce insurance costs through safety awareness programs.
5. Use copy counters.
6. Centralize inventory control.
7. Establish standardized supply lists to take advantage of bulk purchasing.
8. Schedule payrolls so that they do not meet in the bank at the same time.
9. Use U.S. Postal Service library rate, not book rate, for book shipments.
10. Bulk purchase based on standardized supply lists.
11. Offer on a contract basis services to other organizations, such as data processing.
12. Cut phone costs by using an outline as a guide before making a call. Unstructured calls will run up your phone bill.
13. Recycle copier photo paper by using both sides for most in-house documents.
14. Check U.S. Postal Service's monthly memo to mailers containing information on changes in rules and regulations, plus ways to save on mailing costs. For a free subscription, write: Memo Mailers, U.S. Postal Service, Box 999, Springfield, VA 22150.

Facilities and Equipment

1 Institute energy conservation programs.

2 Evaluate in-house vs. outside services; e.g, custodial, printing, etc.

3 Train staff to waste less; e.g., paper supplies, towels, etc.

4 Utilize more efficient procedures or equipment e.g., fewer buses; smaller buses.

5 Use students and staff to clean buildings.

6 Reduce the temperature in the classroom by two degrees in the winter and increase by two degrees in the air-conditioning months.

7 Cut down on unnecessary lighting in cafeteria, gym, chapel, parking lot.

8 Conduct an energy audit.

9 Clean fluorescent tubes every six months and replace after 80 percent of their lamp life.

10 Use dimmer switches where appropriate.

11 Buy diesel buses, which are sturdier and more mileage efficient than conventional buses.

12 Convert school vehicles to natural compressed gas.

13 Cultivate extra land for crops, gardens, or lease to farmers and community.

14 Minimize the use of portable air-conditioning and electric heating units.

15 Use tamper-proof thermostats to avoid frequent changing of the setting.

16 Install automatic door-closing devices.

17 Reduce window glass area, or use double glazed windows.

18 Turn off all electrical equipment when not in use; e.g., computers, typewriters, copy machines.

19 Halogen floodlights offer up to 40 percent energy savings over standard floods - while giving the same light.

20 High pressure sodium, mercury - vapor, or quartz lights are up to seven percent more efficient than incandescent bulbs in outdoor applications.

Instructional

1 Maintain maximum class sizes.

2 Use least expensive means; e.g., ditto vs. copier.

3 Replace long distance field trips with shorter ones.

4 Consider combining grades.

5 Insure that all extracurricular activities pay for themselves.

6 Establish a charge-back system to student activity accounts for indirect staff and material costs.

7 Reschedule kindergarten on three full days a week.

8 Publish list of needed materials and equipment, and circulate the list among vendors.

9 Reduce copying costs by 60 percent by using a Resiograph.

Other

1 Maximize the use of your computer by operating it 24 hours.

2 Properly identify all portable equipment and library books with a security label to discourage stealing.

3 Use U.S. Postal Service library rate rather than book rate.

4 Eliminate use of legal files. Smaller cabinets and file folders are less expensive and save space.

5 Use dividers rather than pendaflex folders.

6 Use low maintenance building materials, textured or decorated wall coverings.

7 Replace across-the-board cuts. It penalizes department heads who already are running a tight ship. The best cuts come from a line-item analysis.

8 Establish partnerships with a few quality vendors, and ask for preferred customer rates. This can easily produce a 3-5 percent savings - and up to 15 percent in some cases.

Maximize the Use of Computer Technology

The advent of the personal computer has made it possible for all Christian schools to accurately establish, monitor and evaluate their financial health.

With the assistance of computer technology, it is much easier to avoid costly over- and under-projections of school income and expenses. Newly developed computer software provides a means whereby schools can anticipate income and expenses given changes in those variables contributing to these changes - changes in fee schedule, tuition rates, family membership, uncollectible tuition, inflation, to name a few.

Given the right software, an administrator can play the "what if" game. What if next year we experience a 2 percent reduction in enrollment? How much would we have to adjust tuition? Or, what if the number of single student families increased by 20? How much could we reduce our tuition so more students could attend? What if we receive a 5 percent increase in outside income, experience a 10 percent reduction in enrollment and a 3 percent increase in teacher salaries? What if we set our base tuition at $1,500 per student? How many students would we need and what composition of students would it take to balance the budget?

What used to take days to calculate can now be accomplished in a matter of a few minutes. Schools with access to a PC computer can contact the authors for copies of a "What If" Lotus spreadsheet package that can be tailor-made for your particular school.

Operate on God's Plan for Financial Success

The financial success of your Christian school is dependent upon the school operating within God's plan for financial success.

Acknowledge That God Owns Everything

> **"The earth is the Lord's, and the fulness thereof; the world, and they that dwell therein"** (Psalm 24:1).

God is the master of the universe. When God manages your school finances, you need not worry. As you transfer ownership of the school building, furnishings, equipment, supplies, books and staff over to God and accept His conditions for control (Deuteronomy 5:32,33.), He will perform His Word by keeping His promises. Every need you have will be provided according to His perfect plan.

> **"But my God shall supply all your need according to his riches in glory in Christ Jesus"** (Philippians 4:19).

Believe it is God's Will for Your School to be Financially Successful

"Beloved, I wish above all things that thou mayest prosper and be in health, even as thy soul prospereth" (3 John 2).

When John penned the words, "Beloved, I wish above all things that thou mayest prosper. . ." the phrase "above all things" indicates that God puts these blessings as top priority above academic success, numerical growth, or athletic accomplishments. God is saying that it is a good thing to have financial success. God wants Christian schools to go beyond the attitude of "just having enough to get by," or "if we could only balance the budget." He wants us to have abundance in every area of the school.

"Now unto him that is able to do exceeding abundantly above all that we ask or think, according to the power that worketh in us" (Ephesians 3:20).

Adopt God's Plan for Blessing

"Therefore I say unto you, What things soever ye desire when ye pray, believe that ye receive them, and ye shall have them" (Mark 11:24).

This is God's pattern for bringing His financial blessing down to your school. Get your attention off from what you think the school should have and onto what the Spirit of God is saying for your school. Allow God's desires to become your desires. Then, believe He will give you the desires of your heart. In this verse, Jesus was simply saying, "You've got to believe you have it (financial success) before you can receive it."

God may have spoken to you to start a Christian school in the middle of an economically-deprived community. All circumstances point to lack. But remember, you are not subject to these conditions, to the curse of lack. Christ has redeemed your school from the curse of impoverished circumstances.

> **"Christ hath redeemed us from the curse of the law, being made a curse for us: for it is written, Cursed is every one that hangeth on a tree:**
>
> **"That the blessing of Abraham might come on the Gentiles through Jesus Christ; that we might receive the promise of the Spirit through faith"** (Galatians 3:13,14).

In fact, God's Word says you are to have dominion over lack. Circumstances are not to dominate you.

> **"For if by one man's offence death reigned by one; much more they which receive abundance of grace and of the gift of righteousness shall reign in life by one, Jesus Christ"** (Romans 5:17).

Poverty is not to rule and reign over your school.

Very often, one will hear parents and students not wanting to come to a Christian school because of what they will have to give up or do without. This is not God's plan. It is an attempt of the enemy to keep schools under the curse. Pastors, administrators, teachers and parents must believe that financial blessings belong to them; all the financial needs of the school are to be satisfied; and that the school should be better than whatever the world's system has to offer. There should be no reason why your Christian children must give up the benefits that the secular school system has to offer in order to attend a Christian school.

You must realize that financial blessing is the plan of God for your school. Dare to believe God for abundance. **". . . I am come that they might have life, and that they might have it more abundantly"** (John 10:10).

The spirit of poverty and lack has no control over a school standing upon the absolute truth of the Word of God.

Other Retention Strategies

10

It is not unusual for schools to experience as high as a 10 percent to 20 percent turnover within a school year and between 20 percent to 40 percent turnover from one academic year to the next. How can a school effectively close the "back door" of student withdrawal?

Retention of students can be improved if taken seriously and a commitment is made to do something about it.

Improve First Impressions

Very few things are as discouraging as seeing students who enter Christian schools for the very first time withdraw at the end of the first week, month, or quarter. Although students and parents may have formed very positive impressions of the school prior to attending, what takes place the first few days and weeks of school either confirms or negates these impressions. Confirmation of positive first impressions will determine the staying influence on students. The following suggestions will help reduce early turnover.

Provide for a Simple Enrollment and Registration Process

The enrollment and registration process are very similar, yet each provides a different function in most schools. During enrollment, students complete application forms, are interviewed, decisions are made for placement and enrollment fees are paid.

The number of students enrolling provides a good indicator of the number of students who will be attending when school starts. Schools use these figures to project budgets, employ staff and purchase resources. Every school experiences situations where parents may have enrolled, but between the time of enrollment and registration, a decision may have been made not to attend for one reason or another. Registration provides an opportunity for the school to really find out how many students are actually coming.

1 **Conduct registration well in advance of the first day of school**. Send out registration information to all those who attended last year, all who are currently enrolled and all students who received an application but have not enrolled. Provide enough time before school starts to followup on all students who were enrolled but did not attend registration.

2 **Create attractive registration packets**. As a special incentive, include fast food coupons from area vendors.

3 **Use plenty of printed signs**. Parents and students need to know where to go and what to do. This leaves the impression of a well-organized school.

4 **Keep it short and simple**. Conduct a review of each enrollee prior to registration to ensure all necessary information is present in their file: authorization for emergency medical treatment; birth certificate; immunization record; health card; transcripts; and any other piece of information to make their file complete. On the day of registration, monitor how long it takes to complete the registration process, and work towards no more than a 30-minute process. Adjust the flow as needed. Have additional staff "on call." Avoid backlogs at all costs.

5 **Insure a warm and friendly environment**. Place your strongest staff monitoring areas where traffic is the heaviest. Provide a refreshment area sponsored by the PTF. Treat every person as a V.I.P. Provide a small gift for everyone in attendance; e.g., pencils, balloons, buttons, book markers, etc.

6 **Provide lots of information**. Each major division of the school should have a special table and key pieces of information; for example:

- **Food services** - school menus;
- **Parent-Teacher Fellowship** - volunteer survey forms;
- **Elementary** - classroom assignments, if known, and supply lists;

- **Athletics** - sport schedules, handbooks and booster club information;
- **Transportation** - zip code listings, bus policies, and car pooling lists;
- **Secondary** - class schedules and course planning sheets;
- **Accounting** - fee schedules and payment plans;
- **Library** - reading lists and book club information.

Provide a Quality New Student Orientation

The basic purpose of orientation is to provide enrolled new students and parents a rapid adjustment to their new school and an early familiarity with school operations. Traditional agendas call for introduction of staff, reviewing special programs, touring the facilities and sharing policies and procedures - all the necessary ingredients for a smooth-flowing orientation, yet boring moments for most children and teenagers.

Very few of the traditional elements of an orientation are going to have a staying influence upon students. Much of what happens during orientation is for the expediency of the school rather than the student. Many of the tasks of an orientation meeting can be accomplished prior to orientation so that orientation is perceived as a relationship building activity. Consider the following suggestions.

Prior Written Communication

Orientation can begin well in advance of the scheduled meeting. Begin with a well-written acceptance and welcome letter from the principal. If it is known what classrooms or homeroom teachers (advisors or counselors) will be assigned, provide this information along with a listing of all teaching staff, degrees earned, teaching experience, hobbies and other items of interest. Provide a list of Parent-Teacher Fellowship officers and student class officers if available. Include a copy of the student handbook and a listing of textbooks to be required. Include a special invitation to visit the school. During the visit, arrange for students to look over the textbooks, visit the science labs, library, etc.

These tasks alone account for more than half of the time spent in traditional orientations. Furthermore, many of the items contained in the handbook can wait until all students are in school. For example, schedule a systematic presentation of the student handbook after the first week of school. Conducting this review in the classroom by teachers provides an opportunity for students to ask questions and to know the "why" behind the way things are done.

Be Creative in Your Program

Accomplish most traditional orientation tasks prior to orientation. This frees the school to focus on creative methods for building enthusiasm, strengthening relationships and forming a bond among students, parents and school staff.

Start the orientation program with a demonstration from the cheerleaders or a teacher skit. Share the vision of the school; point to the future and the success of each student. Include an opportunity to divide larger groups into smaller groups based on grade level; use teachers to head each group.

Take time for introductions of all members of the group; provide opportunity for parents and students to share testimonies of "why they decided to attend your school." Provide time for questions and answers. Conclude with a "Make Your Own Free Sundae" - this is a big winner.

Monitor Transfer Students

Transferring schools, whether from public or private, can be an unsettling experience. Consider using a monthly monitoring instrument that would help identify adjustment problems (See Figure 37).

Assign Strongest Teachers as New Student Advisors

These advisors can be used to establish rapport with students, be the first person a student can turn to for counsel, orientate students to school policy, be a quality and rumor control officer as well as a point for information dissemination. They can administer group tests, career surveys, assist in the scheduling process, evaluate student achievement, and assist students in developing and maintaining self-discipline and study skills. They

INSTRUCTIONS:
1. Student must present form to each teacher and return to Office at end of day.
2. Teachers record comments/initial and return to students after each class.

DAILY BEHAVIOR MONITOR
VICTORY CHRISTIAN SCHOOL
7370 East 71st Street
Tulsa, OK 74133

STUDENT	GRADE
OFFICIAL ISSUING	DATE

PERIOD	ROOM NUMBER	SUBJECT	COMMENTS BEHAVIOR	COMMENTS ACADEMIC EFFORT	TEACHERS INITIAL
HOME ROOM					
1					
2					
3					
4					
5					
6					
7					
8					
9					
10					

FIGURE 37 - Transfer Update

can also be the ones to provide supportive counsel to students returning from suspension or other disciplinary actions. You can increase the effectiveness of the homeroom advisor program by providing for no less than a 15 to 30 minute homeroom period.

Institute an End-of-First-Week Phone Contact

The first thing parents ask when students come home from school is, "How did it go? What happened? How did you like it?" If things are not going great, parents will be the first ones to hear about it. Therefore, have all homeroom teachers and administrators call students at the end of the first week; this provides an opportunity for questions to be resolved, policies and procedures to be clarified and parents and students to know the school cares about them as individuals.

Make Schedule Changes as Soon as Possible

It is not unusual to see upwards of 20 percent of the students wanting schedule changes within the few first days of the opening of school. Traditionally, former students have been given priority.

Instead, allow all students to request schedule changes on a first come, first serve basis.

Set a specific time frame for rescheduling, generally no more than two weeks; require parent approval for all changes; and arrange special after-school and evening rescheduling for parents who work during the day.

Establish a Caring School Climate

Christian educators will agree a positive school climate is important for recruiting and retaining students. The best climate is one where teachers, students and parents can share their concerns openly. This can be facilitated by emphasizing "What is the right thing to do?" rather than "Who is right?" Only after an administrator has gained the trust, confidence and respect of the students, teachers and parents, will he be effective in bringing about change.

Provide Explanations

When students and parents form opinions based on second-hand information, it may be a sign the school needs to provide more explanations for decisions affecting students and parents. For example, try reducing a student lunch hour by five minutes so there would be less need for teacher supervision. You guessed it, problems! You will end up having to explain "why" in very much detail to every high school student and his parents. Sharing with people "why" decisions are made may not lead to everyone being in agreement, but people will be satisfied their opinions were heard.

Why don't administrators share the "why" of decisions? Could it be there is a fear of losing control over the results? Is it a lack of confidence in the ability of parents and students to understand?

Thank God, He has not given administrators a spirit of fear, but of power, love, and a sound mind (2 Timothy 1:7). Using your sound mind,

1 Provide a reason for the decision.

2 Explain the decision by using every communication tool at your disposal.

3 Specify the results that you expect to see obtained by this decision.
4 Provide for questions and answers.

Be Understanding and Supportive of Staff

"The schoolhouse must be a kind of home which offers its inhabitants a sense of belonging, of individuality strengthened by expectation, of security born of respect" (Peters and Austin, 1985, p. 468).

It is important for the school to have a strong home base before it can effectively reach out to recruit and retain students. "To try to build understanding, acceptance and support of your organization in the community without having achieved it inside your organization with your own employees is obviously a losing approach. One reason is that the community relations cannot, through clever communications to the community, cover up a weak product or poor employee situation at home" (Yarrington, 1983, p. 153).

Understanding and support can be fostered in staff by:

1 Rewarding teachers for professional development.
2 Meeting their financial needs.
3 Recognizing a job well done and those who are trying new procedures.
4 Providing adequate supplies, materials and physical setting.
5 Providing opportunity for staff to contribute ideas (providing lip service is a disaster).
6 Maintaining management consistency.
7 Fostering a commitment to the established vision.

Staff need to feel they are needed and an important asset to the school. Such feelings produce high expectations, promote employee satisfaction and loyalty. This leads to quality services to students and parents. As a result, teachers become enthusiastic recruiters.

Enforce Fair and Consistent Discipline Policies

Over the past 15 years, parents have pointed to discipline as the top issue facing public schools. It is for this reason that many parents seek a Christian school placement. Likewise, lack of discipline and inconsistent enforcement of existing rules could lead parents to withdraw from Christian schools.

One of the greatest frustrations facing parents who enroll for the first time in a Christian school is a false assumption that there will be few discipline challenges. Parents need to be made aware that just as children are at a different level of spiritual maturity, they will be at different levels of self-discipline. But, regardless of the level, students need to be held accountable for their behavior.

Teachers, in turn, need to establish themselves in the classroom as the authority and hold students accountable for school work, good behavior and living consistent, Christ-like lives. This leads to gaining the respect of students and parents. So when the teacher speaks, the students listen and heed the teacher's words. When students hear and obey their teacher, they will hear and obey the Spirit of God. Strong schools are built on teachers who foster strong discipline.

Teachers and students need to be trained to be sensitive to the convicting power of the Holy Spirit to such a degree that the slightest conduct that grieves the Holy Spirit will be evidenced in the teacher's and student's spirit (inner man). Obedience to the prompting of the Holy Spirit results in classroom peace and harmony.

Many times what teachers see as discipline challenges is little more than the outward manifestation of an inward conflict that has a spiritual basis, such as rebellion. Schools need to train teachers to deal with the behavior (symptom), but also to take authority over the spirit (source).

> **"For we wrestle not against flesh and blood, but against principalities, against powers, against the rulers of the darkness of this world, against spiritual wickedness in high places"** (Ephesians 6:12).

When teachers learn to manage the spirit of the student rather than the behavior, the behavior changes to match the spirit (See *Spirit-Directed Discipline* by the authors).

Target Challenge Students

Identify a list of questionable students, and assign a particular staff person who could best minister to the needs of the students and parents. Have them conduct an individual meeting with the student and a parent conference. In most cases, if the school can help resolve a student's questions, this resolve will be a positive influence to his parents.

Improve Recognition Programs

Establish a comprehensive program of student recognition, using programs such as student of the week, month, quarter, semester, year-grade level, or by classroom; provide for godly character awards and honor rolls (See Schindler, 1987, for a complete awards program).

Offer all students a special privilege card as a reward, such as outstanding achievement. Award honor students with a honors card. Include benefits like several days of early release from school, excused from wearing the school uniform as long as they are in dress clothes, late arrival to school, etc.

Use special announcements, banners, or bulletin boards to recognize students. Provide school jackets and lettering for academics, fine arts, as well as the performing arts.

Each point of recognition or award provides a personal positive attachment to the school.

Improve Student Morale with Assemblies

Include a wide variety of inspiring, informative programs for assemblies. Christian schools have rigorous chapel schedules; they also need to consider presenting assemblies that provide variety and entertainment, yet relay a spiritual message. Using students in planning and conducting assemblies makes the students feel assemblies are theirs, not just something the school staff has planned. Consider assemblies for subgroups within the student body, such as all freshmen, seniors, juniors and the like.

The value of assemblies is important for it allows the entire student body or large groups to come together for educational and recreational purposes. Properly planned, organized, and directed assemblies can have a major impact on student retention.

It doesn't take long for the news of dynamic and fulfilling assemblies and chapels to spread throughout the church community.

Improve Teacher Image and Parent Interactions

Most educators will agree, the teacher plays a crucial role in student retention. "Who will be my teachers?" This is one of the most important questions asked by students and parents considering enrolling (re-enrolling) in your school. Essential to a quality program is the teacher who is caring, creative, hard-working, friendly, enthusiastic and interested in learning.

Teachers who attract students are those who have an inner excitement about life in general and the Gospel in particular. Those teachers who display zeal and excitement grounded in the Scriptures will have a magnetic effect upon students and parents.

When teachers display aliveness, are bright, and optimistic, their teaching will be interesting, student response will be stimulated, communication will flow, and students will continue to return year after year.

Sometimes, without knowing, staff can treat parents as an impediment. For example, a teacher who is so busy clearing off her desk that no one greets a parent who just walked in. Teachers need to view parents and students not as interruptions, but as blessings - they are the reason the school exists.

Teachers can have a positive effect upon parents by:

1. Returning phone calls promptly.
2. Being receptive to what parents have to say.
3. Approaching every meeting with a parent by asking, "How can I best minister and meet the need(s) of this family"?
4. Ministering reconciliation, love, acceptance and forgiveness.
5. Using positive expressions rather than negative expressions when speaking to parents about their children - "Can do more when he tries" rather than "He is lazy," "Should learn to work with others" rather than "Uncooperative," "Could make better use of time" rather than "Wastes time."
6. Showing parents the school is concerned about their children by scheduling conferences both during the day and evening

hours, providing day care sitting services and coordinating conferences for all children on the same day.

7 Using praise calls or notes concerning their children to overcome negative images about school conferences.

8 Being courteous.

Peters and Austin (1985) in their best seller, *A Passion for Excellence*, indicate the success of Disney parks, McDonald's, and IBM goes beyond location, cleanliness and uniform standards and quality products; success is a direct result of common courtesy and good service. Consider the following strengthening options.

Modify Instructional Systems

Most Christian schools have very strong academic programs. Academics are enhanced by a strong instructional system: a must for student retention.

Help Students be Successful

Programs and opportunities designed to assist students develop to their full potential have a powerful influence on retention.

1 Provide a system of assistance with current class assignments.

2 Provide tools to help them get organized for study. Place a copy of a *Student Study and Assignment Guide* in the hands of every student, grades 1-8th.

3 Offer tutorial assistance in mathematics, language arts and science. Students tutoring other students can lead to improved academic achievement for both student and tutor and to positive attitudes toward course work.

The most successful programs are those that are highly structured, well-planned and last for a relatively short duration, generally a few weeks or months. Tutorial assistance is important especially for the student who may hesitate to re-enroll, knowing the school's academic average is 1-2 grades above public school norms.

4 Purchase computer-based remedial programs (See Skillbank II).

5 Present workshops on techniques for taking standardized tests. Add a SAT preparatory course, and require all high school

teachers to include SAT and ACT preparation material as part of the ongoing curricula.

6 Offer more independent study programs.

7 Teach and train students how to study. Offer the *POWER* series study curriculum to all students grades 7-9th.

8 Establish a communication link with administrators or counselors when students believe they have challenges with teachers.

9 Provide a homework hot line. (Contact the authors for a sample foundation application requesting funding for a Home-to-School Based Communication System. Your local phone company may fund such a request.)

Provide a Variety of Course Offerings

It is very difficult for students who are college bound to take more than the standard courses or specialty courses, such as homemaking, art, music, or industrial arts.

One solution is to reduce the amount of time in each period and add an extra period to the schedule; another is to add an option of attending special classes scheduled either before or after the standard school day such as before and after school computer labs. Offer computers two days per week for elementary and three days for secondary students.

Consider offering three levels of graduation diplomas:

- **DIPLOMA** for those students who meet the basic state standards.
- **MERIT** for those students who meet the credits required by your Christian school.
- **HONORS** for those students who meet the school's credits and have taken no less than four accelerated or honors courses and have attained a GPA of 3.5 and higher.

Keep Parents Informed of Academic Progress

Consider moving the nine-week reporting periods to three, six- and nine-weeks. This would help teachers stay current with grades and provide more accurate and up-to-date reporting of performance to parents.

There is nothing more frustrating to parents than to hear at the end of the first nine weeks their son or daughter is failing, and there is little hope of improving the quarter grade (See Columbia Computer Systems for a comprehensive academic, attendance, scheduling and student records computer system).

Strengthen College Admissions Preparation

Improving college admissions preparation can be accomplished by providing high schoolers a college preparation handbook. It may be possible to obtain the assistance of a local vocational school, junior college, college or university to underwrite the cost of this publication for permission to include information on their institutions in the handbook.

Focus first on those post high school institutions that most of your graduates attend. A sample copy of such a handbook is available on a computer disk, ready to be modified to fit your particular school situation. Contact the authors for more information.

Communicate Your Christian Philosophy of Education

Every Christian school has had parents who have withdrawn their children, placing them back in secular school. This decision may have been based on any number of stated reasons:

- Lack of finances.
- Unresolvable differences.
- Less than adequate facilities.
- Sub-standard curriculum.
- Doctrinal variations.

Very seldom does a parent attribute withdrawal to an inadequate understanding of the philosophy of Christian education.

Given a full understanding of the philosophy behind Christian education, parents would seek out another Christian school, or home schooling, rather than returning their child to secular school.

In addressing the issue of Christian education in the 90's, David Hand (1991), Associate Director of the Oral Roberts

University Educational Fellowship (ORUEF) and Chairman of the International Christian Accreditation Association (ICAA) said,

> "The challenge we will continue to face . . . is the need to communicate the Christian school message more effectively" (p. 2).

David L. Roth (1984), in *Administration of the Christian School*, said,

> "Educating our parents as to the purpose and objectives of the Christian school is a major undertaking" (p. 128).

Preference Verses Conviction

Given two choices, secular or Christian schooling, most Christian parents would prefer Christian schooling. They prefer to surround their children with wholesome friends, teachers who will go the extra mile, quality academics, disciplined classrooms and an enriched spiritual atmosphere. Unfortunately, some parents place their children in a Christian school for reasons that will not stand the test of conflict, dissatisfaction, financial pressure and a whole host of other forces.

Our experience has shown that approximately 60 percent of those parents enrolling their children in Christian schools do so for superficial reasons - very few make any reference to a philosophy of Christian education.

Enrollment decisions not based on a strong Christian education philosophy will lead parents to withdraw their children when faced with situations where there seems to be no acceptable solutions. For example, how many of us have heard the excuses, "I'd like to keep my children in school, but with finances as they are, it'll be better for our family if we send them back to public school." "I know my son should be a better student. Why he continues to be so undisciplined I don't know. You have done all I can expect of a school. We prefer to go ahead and enroll him back in public school where he can be with all of his friends and with those teachers who really know him." Each of these decisions is based on preferences and no conviction for Christian education.

Christian educators need to instill in their parents convictions, not preferences, for Christian education. Viewing Christian education as "just another alternative" shows a lack of awareness of the whole concept of Christian education. Convictions founded on a strong philosophy of Christian education will lead parents to conclude, "Keeping Johnny in your Christian school doesn't look financially feasible, but we're going to believe God for extra finances so he can stay in your school. There aren't any other Christian schools in town; home schooling is not an option. There's no way he's going to return to public school!"

Strong convictions for Christian education are what causes pastors to go to jail rather than close their Christian school; convictions motivate young people to give up their Saturday at the beach in favor of marching in front of a health clinic, protesting abortion. A conviction of love and compassion led Christ to the cross. He would have preferred to let the cup pass from Him and for God to come up with another way to handle sin; nevertheless, Jesus was obedient unto death.

Convictions are what move parents to believe God for the necessary finances, to approach teachers and administrators - speaking the truth in love, and to help improve programs rather than preferring not to get involved, or not to "ruffle anyone's feathers." Preference leads to copout, while conviction leads to commitment.

Knowledge as a Foundation

A strong philosophy of education with conviction must be built on a foundation of knowledge. Hosea 4:6 warns, "**My people are destroyed for lack of knowledge...**" Without proper knowledge things seem senseless.

Presenting all the knowledge needed to build a solid philosophy of Christian education is beyond the scope of this book. (The authors are presently working on a book titled *Spirit-Directed Model of Education*, soon to be released, which will take readers beyond Christian education as an alternative to secular education and presents God's original intention for education.) Rather, we would like to present some workable suggestions on how schools might better communicate their philosophy of Christian education to their parents and students.

Write Your Philosophy of Christian Education

Communicate the vision of the school by writing it down, placing it on an audio or video tape. Require each family enrolling to listen to and be in agreement with the vision. "**And the LORD answered me, and said, Write the vision, and make it plain upon tables, that he may run that readeth it**" (Habakkuk 2:2).

Present a written copy of the school's philosophy of Christian education first to the staff, then to the parents. In courses we have taught for Christian school teachers and administrators, seven out of every ten have no written philosophy. They may be able to tell us about how they teach, but they have never taken the time to write it down. When it is written down, distributed to staff and parents, the school can be held accountable; its "talked" about philosophy of Christian education must be congruent with its "working" philosophy. When this happens, there is a unity that attracts parents and their children.

Use Audio-Visual Media

Most parents have not seen the big picture; they are not aware of the influence of secular humanism on our nation's schools. Many parents have a false assumption; they feel if their children go to church, believe in the Bible, and attend Sunday school, they will be immune to humanism. Show the video, "Let Their Eyes be Open"(1975) and "Taking Liberties: The Legacy of the ACLU" (1990). Contact ORUEF for these two Videos.

Require every parent to read pamphlets, such as: "Have You Enrolled Your Children In Christian School For The Right Reasons" (Kienel, 1989) and "Christian School Education: No Longer An Option" (Demuth, 1983).

Develop a Philosophy Brochure

Provide parents with an attractive brochure outlining God's mandate for education and training. Use Scriptures from the Amplified Bible;

- Proverbs 1:7.
- Deuteronomy 6:1-9,17,22; 11:18-23.
- Psalm 78:1-8.
- Jeremiah 10:1-2.

- Isaiah 54:13.
- Colossians 2:3,8-11.
- Matthew 18:6.
- Proverbs 19:27.

Knowing what God's Word has to say about teaching and training provides a foundation upon which parents can release their faith. For example,

> **"Father, Your Word says my children should not learn the way of the heathen; rather, I should train them up in the way they should go. You say they are to cease from learning the instruction that causes them to err from the words of knowledge. Father, I am asking You to help provide a way to enroll and keep them in a Christian school."**

Allow the entire uncompromised Word of God to be brought to bear against those forces and situations keeping children out of Christian schools. Find the Scripture verse that applies, and declare it over the particular situation.

For example, when faced with a financial situation, the world says, "Hold on to every dollar, tighten your belt, withdraw your children." God's Word says, "**Give, and it shall be given unto you; good measure, pressed down, and shaken together, and running over, shall men give into your bosom. For with the same measure that ye mete withal it shall be measured to you again**" (Luke 6:38). Help your parents to be givers of their money, time and talent.

We have found one of the best ways for parents to get an extra job is to begin giving by volunteering at the school or church. God honors their commitment, and when faith is put alongside their effort, their need is met. Adhering to the truth in God's Word brings victory over every situation.

Sponsor An Essay Contest

Invite parents to place in writing their own words to the question: "Why do I believe in Christian education?"

Appoint a review team of staff and parents to read the essays and select the best three. Offer the top winners, one from each division of the school (K-3, 4-6, 7-8, 9-12), a free dinner for two, tuition reduction for one month, free books, etc. Publish the top essays and place them in your information packets.

Use Your Newsletter

Feature a series on Christian school philosophy. Use excepts from "Educational Research Analysts Newsletter," "Capsule," and other Christian school literature.

Include Philosophy Issues in Pulpit Sermons

Encourage the pastor to include Christian philosophy in his sermons. Topics like Evolution vs. Creation, the New Age Movement, American Background of Freedom will be well received. It is the pastor's responsibility to educate his congregation on these important issues. Pastor Billy Joe Daugherty has been very instrumental in presenting these issues from the pulpit. (Contact Victory Books and Tapes, 1-918-493-1700, for a listing of available cassette tapes). Whenever he preaches on one of these topics or includes information on Christian schools in his sermon, one can expect the school information table to be packed.

On the day the sermon is delivered, prepare a special bulletin announcement of the topic, and have a detailed outline of the topic available at the school information table.

Invite special speakers, such as David Barton, speaker on our Christian heritage, to present the Christian view of education to your school, church and community - 817-441- 6044.

Offer Special Sunday School Classes

There is nothing like a captivated audience to impart Christian philosophy. Offer a short mini course as part of the Sunday school curriculum. Add some variety by including a debate, special speakers, such as teachers, students and parents who are on fire about Christian education. Use the book by LaHaye (1982), *The Battle for the Family*.

Contact other Sunday school departments. Review their curriculum and see where they might insert information on the philosophy of Christian education. This is easiest in adult classes dealing with the family as well as in high school classes.

Build a Professional Library

Circulate copies of "*Weep for Your Children*" by Murray Norris. Build a professional and parent library with the following books. Include a five-minute book review during your regularly scheduled Parent-Teacher Fellowship.

- *Educating for Eternity* by Claude E.Schindler and Pacheco Pyle
- *Reasons for Sending Your Child to a Christian School* by Paul A. Kienel
- *Are Textbooks Harming our Children* by James C. Hefley
- *Four Trojan Horses of Humanism* by Harry Conn
- *The Philosophy of Christian School Education* by Paul A. Kienel, Ed.
- *The Battle for Public Schools* by Tim LaHaye
- *Education that is Christian* by Lois E. LeBar
- *To Christian School Parents* by Roy W. Lowrie, Jr.

Foster a God-Centered Total Life View

Since much of what parents learn is a direct reflection of what their children are learning, take the responsibility of showing the relevance of the Bible and Christian philosophy to each and every phase of school life. Give your students (thus your parents) a total life view with God at the center - a view that measures all of life against Biblical standards

Other Retention Ideas

Establish a Re-enrollment Committee

Often, the committee approach is viewed as an ineffective organization. However, a re-enrollment committee will work for you if you work it. Here are some suggestions:

1. Appoint parents to serve on the committee.
2. Set specific enrollment and re-enrollment goals.
3. Don't allow one single family to fall through the cracks.
4. Keep good records, including a listing of reasons parents give for not re-enrolling.

5 Develop a written response to be mailed to all who indicated they would not be returning.

6 Place all non-returning parents (students) on a follow-up tickler system.

When re-enrolling students, use the KISS formula - Keep IT Short and Simple. The less paperwork required, the better.

Use Homeroom Teachers

Make each teacher responsible for re-enrolling his/her homeroom class. No more than two weeks after parents receive their re-enrollment packets, ask teachers to call the parents of their homeroom students who have not been enrolled.

This effort must be closely coordinated to avoid multiple calls to families with more than one student in school. Create a tabulation system to track each call as well as parent responses. The goal of every teacher is to work towards enrolling every student in their homeroom. Also, have them call those already enrolled and commend them for making this decision early.

Pre-schedule Students

The mere fact students have next year's schedule completed provides a significant incentive for re-enrolling. Providing high school students with a computerized graduation status report affords an additional retention link to the school. Some computer programs, such as that provided by Columbia, allows schools to establish a new scheduling any time after school begins. Computerized scheduling can reduce the time taken to produce schedules. Pre-scheduling should be done no later than April for the next school term.

In the elementary grades, students should be given an opportunity to spend a few hours in the next grade level during your re-enrollment period. Call it the New Horizons Day. Teachers welcome students to the next grade level and point to the new and exciting things that will be happening next year. Invariably, students will go home at the end of the day, begging Mom and Dad to re-enroll them.

Use Student Recruiters

Using specially trained students to assist other students, although they are not expected to address and remediate all the causes of attrition, can help students resolve dissatisfaction, lack of commitment, friendship, peer group influences and study behaviors.

The influence of peers to promote retention draws upon the natural influence and bonding which exists between members of the peer group. Besides, students are more willing to seek out and accept advice and direction from other students, because they share common school experiences.

Provide Before- and After-school Child Care

Providing a quality before- and after-school child care program is an attractive recruiting consideration. Victory Christian School provides such a program titled, Victory Activities (See Appendix P). The program includes first through sixth graders. Another program titled, Victory Extended Day, is an attempt to offer a full day kindergarten program for working parents. The number of hours children are maintained is just under the legal limit so as not to be licensed as a day care.

If you are limited for space and unable to establish after school and extended day programs, look for the nearest available program offering these services. Provide transportation services between the two locations so parents can pick their family up at one location. Properly managed, these programs can make a comfortable financial contribution to the school.

Give Your Handbook a Face Lift

Look for creative ways of saying the same thing. Student handbooks go either ignored after their initial distribution or are referred to so seldom that their publication costs are difficult to justify.

Consider the following:

1 Placing the most important message to be communicated at the very front of the handbook.

2 Replacing mimeographed typewritten material with desktop published material and laser printed text. Include bold headlines, graphics and pictures.
3 Place vendor coupons on various pages.
4 Use footers at the bottom of each page, such as quotes from former students.
5 Print numbers in each handbook to be used for the first four weeks to conduct special drawings for prizes, such as a large pizza delivered at noon hour.
6 Provide pages for students to record the master timetable.
7 Add address and phone number pages.
8 Include a short biographical sketch of staff and class officers.
9 Use a reproduction of the yearbook cover as a cover, or one designed by students.
10 Include a place to record the names, addresses and phone numbers of all teachers.

A well-designed handbook communicates a message of confidence, efficiency and foresight; it establishes an organized, substantial academic and social environment.

Retention of students can be improved if taken seriously and a commitment made to do something about it.

A Final Word

11

God has a specific plan for your school. "'**For I know the plans I have for you,' declares the Lord, 'plans to prosper you and not to harm you, plans to give you hope and a future**'" (Jeremiah 29:11, NIV). Furthermore, God says, "**I will instruct you and teach you in the way you should go; I will counsel you and watch over you**" (Psalm 32:8, NIV).

Planning involves identifying objectives, selecting strategies, developing action plans and evaluating the results.

Identify Objectives

If you recall the story of Alice in Wonderland, you will remember she was lost. In coming to a fork in the road, she saw a cat in a tree. She asked the cat, "Which road should I take?" The cat replied, "Where do you want to go?" Alice said, "I don't know." The cat responded, "Well then, any road will get you there."

A goal gives direction; it is always measurable and attainable within a given period of time. Without a measurable goal, you will never know whether or not your recruiting and retention efforts are successful.

Myron Rush (1983) in *Management: A Biblical Approach* said,

> "Without measurable objectives, people tend to talk and plan in generalities. They profess to be 'trusting God to lead,' but do not know where they are headed and are unable to determine when they have arrived. On the other hand, measurable objectives focus on exactly what one believes God will do, how much a person is trusting God for, and when it will occur. Measurable objectives bring

faith into focus, giving it meaning and an identity" (p. 86).

For example, in 1985, Victory Christian School established the following objectives as part of a five-year plan (See Table 7):

TABLE 7 - Key Results

Key Result Area	Year				
	85-86	86-87	87-88	88-89	89-90
Enrollment will be	625	680	725	780	825
% of students from VCC	40	60	62	65	70
% enrolled will be remain enrolled	76	80	83	85	90

Select Strategies

Once the objectives have been set, strategies can be selected. Prayerfully consider every strategy suggested in this book. Start out with several strategies; then narrow these down to the ones which best match your particular situation.

Victory's objective of expecting 70 percent of its students to be Victory members led to a strategy of providing a 50 percent discount for active church members. This resulted in a 20 percent increase in church members attending the very first year it was implemented.

Formulate an Action Plan

Once the strategies have been selected, the next step requires formulation of a detailed action plan for each strategy.

1 **Place each selected strategy in proper sequence**. The right strategy performed at the wrong time can be less productive. For example, Victory used to advertise at various times during the day in the summer months. While in prayer, the Holy Spirit quickened us to focus our radio advertising during the

week of Kenneth Hagin's Campmeeting and have the spots run 60 minutes before and after the service. Every year, since this change was made, six to ten students have been enrolled as a result of this specific strategy.

2 **Identify time lines for the completion of each strategy**. For example, ten rotating radio spots will be completed by July 10. Spots will be played in rotation with two spots per hour from 7 a.m. to 9 a.m., 4 p.m. to 6 p.m., Monday through Friday, from August 9 through August 13.

3 **Identify resources**. Identify and allocate appropriate resources necessary to carry out the strategies; these resources include: people, equipment, supplies and finances.

Evaluate the Results

Following through on each action plan should lead to accomplishing each strategy. When all strategies are completed, the objective should be accomplished.

The qualitative changes taking place through the implementation of the various strategies should result in quantitative changes: more students recruited and a higher retention percentage.

Rating scales, surveys and questionnaires can be used to measure qualitative changes, while numbers and statistical data provide an objective measure of the overall quantitative effectiveness of the recruiting and retaining efforts much like the box scores in baseball producing the "runs, hits, and errors" of the game.

As each strategy is implemented, it is monitored to determine if it is moving the school towards its objective. Often, a strategy that looks good on the planning board fails to produce the desired results. When this happens, adjustment must be instituted or new strategies identified until the objective is reached.

Have Confidence in God's Call

If your school is going through a period of shrinking enrollment, or if you experience this in the future, we have a special word for you. "The situations you are facing today, or will face in the future, may lead you to question God's call to raise up a Christian school, or even to serve as the administrator. Expect these circumstances, whether they concern students, staff, programs, facilities, or finances to line up with God's calling."

God has called your Christian school to be successful - developing toward full maturity." Consider these verses:

> **"And those he predestined, he also called; those he called, he also justified; those he justified, he also glorified"** (Romans 8:30, NIV).
>
> **"God, who has called you into fellowship with his Son Jesus Christ our Lord, is faithful"** (1 Cor 1:9, NIV).
>
> **"But to those whom God has called, both Jews and Greeks, Christ the power of God and the wisdom of God"** (I Cor 1:24, NIV).
>
> **"For you know that we dealt with each of you as a father deals with his own children, encouraging, comforting and urging you to live lives worthy of God, who calls you into his kingdom and glory"** (1 Thes 2:11, NIV).
>
> **"He called you to this through our gospel, that you might share in the glory of our Lord Jesus Christ"** (2 Thes 2:14, NIV).
>
> **"His divine power has given us everything we need for life and godliness through our knowledge of him who called us by his own glory and goodness"** (2 Pet 1:3, NIV).
>
> **"Therefore, my brothers, be all the more eager to make your calling and election sure. For if you do these things, *you will never fall*"** (2 Pet 1:10, NIV).

When you have confidence in God's calling, you will have confidence in dealing with any situation blocking His plan from being fulfilled.

God's plan calls for bringing into existence a new breed of Christian schools, ones to help usher in the return of Christ. In these schools are students training to be mighty men and women used by God for signs and wonders.

> **"Behold, I and the children whom the Lord hath given me are for signs and for wonders. . ."** (Isaiah 8:18).

These students are to be examples in word, love, spirit, faith and purity. They will go forth in boldness to do the works of Jesus - healing the brokenhearted, bringing deliverance, recovering sight to the blind, setting at liberty those that are bruised, casting out devils, speaking with new tongues, laying hands on the sick; and having power over the enemy (Luke 4:18, 10:19; Mark 16:17; 1 John 5:14).

They are to be ten times better than students educated under the world's educational system. Daniel 1:20 says,

> **"And in all matters of wisdom and understanding, that the king inquired of them, he found them ten times better than all the magicians and astrologers that were in all his realm."**

Believe God's Promises

God's word for you is found in Romans 4:20,21:

> **"He staggered not at the promise of God through unbelief; but was strong in faith, giving glory to God;**
>
> **"And being fully persuaded that, what he had promised, he was also able to perform."**

Second Peter 1:4 states,

> **"Whereby are given unto us exceeding great and precious promises. . ."**

Moses (Red Sea), the three Hebrew children (fiery furnace), David (Goliath), Daniel (lions), Joshua (Jericho), Gideon (Midianites) and Jesus (Calvary), all faced overwhelming circumstances. But in every situation, they believed what God had promised. There was no variance in their belief. They all came out on top.

Peter took his eyes off Jesus, looked at his circumstances, doubted and began to sink. Unbelief is what causes sinking and staggering. These come when the mind tries to reason away what God said; doubt is almost always based on words of others and past experiences rather than on the Word of God.

Negative words spoken become directors of doubt - "I don't think it will work; the school will never increase in enrollment; we've tried that strategy before and it'll never work; we can never afford it; or we don't have any resources."

The words that are spoken should be those based on what God has said - His Word. Declaring the Word of God over circumstances and situations builds faith that activates our "persuader" - it causes us to be persuaded that those things He has spoken about your school, He is able to bring them to pass. You can be persuaded in the following:

1. No weapon formed against me and our school shall prosper, and every tongue that shall rise against me in judgment I shall condemn. This is my heritage (Isaiah 54:17).
2. I delight myself in the Lord and He gives me the desires of my heart (Psalm 37:4).
3. There is no lack in our school for my God supplies all of our needs according to His riches in glory by Christ Jesus (Philippians 4:19).
4. In all my ways and the ways of the school, I acknowledge Him and He directs my path (Proverbs 3:6).

Let God be in Charge

Second Corinthians 2:14 says, "**Now thanks be unto God, which always causeth us to triumph in Christ...**" Settle it in your mind. **Always** is normal with God. If God is causing you to triumph, you never will fail. Never accept defeat as the final verdict, no matter what it looks like or how you feel. Hold fast your profession of faith without wavering (Hebrews 10:23). God will bring you out on top.

Vince Lombardi, when asked about losing a game said, "We didn't lose, we just ran out of time."

Since it is God who causes you to triumph, He personally accepts responsibility for your victory. God never runs out of time - we do. **DON'T QUIT UNTIL YOU WIN!**

Listen to and Obey the Spirit of God

Acknowledge the fact: God is Lord over your life and your school. God wants you and your school to be successful more than you want them to be successful.

There are some who feel that every calamity, every bad situation that comes to their life and the school has been put there by God to test their faith. God is not the author of these things. God's desire is for your school to succeed. It is the devil who comes to close down Christian schools; the devil comes to steal, kill, and destroy (John 10:10). He is the one who would like nothing better than to see your school close its doors.

The Holy Spirit Directs Your Paths

There are many practical suggestions in this book. The Holy Spirit will confirm the ones that your school should implement.

In Proverbs 16:9 it says, "**A man's heart deviseth his way: but the Lord directeth his steps.**" In the Amplified, it says, "**A man's mind plans his way, but the Lord directs his steps and makes them sure.**"

God's desire is for your steps to be blessed, victorious, triumphant; these steps include full enrollment.

Proverbs 3:5,6 says,

> **"Trust in the Lord with all thine heart; and lean not unto thine own understanding.**

"In all thy ways acknowledge him, and he shall (not will, if he chooses, or someday He might) **direct thy paths."**

Acknowledge the facts:

1. He is in charge of your enrollment.
2. He is Lord over your programs.
3. He is in charge of teacher hiring.
4. He is the chief Admissions Officer.
5. He is Lord over all the curriculum.
6. He is Lord over student activities.

When you say this, God says, "I will direct thy steps." This means God will cause you to walk in the right path - to make the right decisions, to be at the right place doing the right thing, in the right way, at the right time.

His directing your steps comes by trusting in your heart. The only way to trust in your heart (your spirit) is through an inward witness of the Spirit of God.

The Holy Spirit Speaks to You and Shows You Things to Come

> **"Howbeit when he, the Spirit of truth, is come, he will guide you into all truth; for he shall not speak of himself; but whatsoever he shall hear, that shall he speak: and he will shew you things to come"** (John 16:13).

God is going to take care of your school's future.

> **"For I know the thoughts that I think toward you, saith the Lord, thoughts of peace, and not of evil, to give you an expected end"** (Jeremiah 29:11).

God is doing everything to reveal His will for your school. He wants you to know His master plan. Once you believe God wants you to know His will, you are well on your way, for God has an avenue of faith through which He can speak to you.

When you became a Christian, God came in you. You became the righteousness of God in Christ Jesus (2 Corinthians 5:21). Your body became the temple of the Holy Spirit (1 Corinthians 6:19). The steps of a righteous person are ordered of the Lord. If God said your steps are ordered, then they are. Accepting this truth builds confidence in the decisions you are making.

First John 5:14,15 says,

> **"And this is the confidence we have in him, that, if we ask any thing according to his will, he heareth us:**
>
> **"And if we know that he hear us, whatsoever we ask, we know that we have the petitions that we desired of him."**

Jeremiah 33:3 exhorts us to:

"Call unto me, and I will answer thee and show thee great and mighty things..."

God said, *you ask*, and *I'll show*! What do you want to know about your school? God said He would give you an answer.

Expect Change

The only thing that isn't subject to change is God.

"For I am the LORD, I change not..." (Malachi 3:6).

Jesus said of Peter, **"Thou art...thou shalt be..."** (John 1:42). Peter failed, but Jesus had an image of the possibilities in Peter's life.

You may feel you've made some serious mistakes and are far from perfection. Don't look back at your failures in dealing with students, parents and programs.

John Mason (1990) in his book, *An Enemy Called Average*, said,

> "When you refuse to change; you end up in chains... When we are called upon by the Lord to change, we will continue to reach toward the same goal, but perhaps in a slightly different way. When we refuse to cooperate with the change that God is requiring of us, we make chains constrain and restrict us... We should choose not to allow the way we've always done it to cause us to miss opportunities God is providing for us today" (pp.71,72).

Look to God to show you how your school must change. Maybe it's in relationship to your position on home schooling, tuition collections, or student activities. Isaiah said,

"See, the former things have taken place, and new things I declare; before they spring into being I announce them to you" (Isaiah 42:9, NIV).

Expect each day to bring a new level of wisdom, understanding and knowledge to your administrative responsibilities.

Each day expect to move toward God's idea of what your school is to be.

A school that doesn't change falls to mediocrity. This eventually leads to compromise, "We'll do anything, just don't withdraw your children from school," or "Well, just this one time." A school that begins to compromise standards for higher enrollment will multiply its challenges and lose its dynamic effect upon students and the community.

Have a Passion for Improvement

Paul said, "**I press toward the mark. . .**" (Philippians 3:14). This is much different than competition against another school which happens between sport teams. A passion for improvement measures your school where it is now and where it will be tomorrow.

A declining enrollment can be reversed when a school seeks improvement stemming from a Spirit-directed motive to please God rather than to follow a list of suggestions as a form of compliance.

Someone once said, "Every outstanding success is built upon ability and eagerness to do better than 'good enough.'"

Ninety-nine percent quality isn't good enough. Motorola's target is 99.9999998 percent defect free production among the computer chips and electronic parts it makes. The company says a 99 percent quality rate is nowhere near good enough. With 99 percent performance, hospital workers would accidentally drop 30,000 newborn babies each year.

Every school wants to have a maximum enrollment. To reach this success goal means putting forth the extra effort - "the only place success is found without effort is in the dictionary."

We're reminded of the little five year old who was struggling with a heavy table when her mother came along and said, "Bonnie, you can't move that table. It's too big for you."

Bonnie responded, "Yes, I can. See, I'm as tall as it is. So, I guess I ought to be able to move it if I want to."

You have to have the "want to." What is your level of determination? There is nothing too big to undertake when you measure it alongside your determination and faith in the God of possibilities.

Be careful not to fall in the trap of wanting more students so you can have bigger and better programs, so you can have more students, so you can have bigger and better programs, so you can... etc. A school needs to focus on changing students' lives and moving them to Christ likeness.

The KEY to recruiting and retaining students is having a quality Christian school that goes beyond just building enrollment: a school preparing an end-time army to do the works of Jesus.

This last page is just the beginning! Throughout the reading of this book, the Holy Spirit has been working in your spirit and on your mind - identifying areas needing immediate attention, pointing out those strategies that best match your particular situation and giving you creative ideas not even mentioned in this book. Take the time, even now, to write these down.

What the Spirit of God is Saying to me:

References

ADVO-Systems, Inc., 2727 E. 21st, #100, Tulsa, OK 74114. Phone Gary Haynes, 918-743-8967.

Baker, A.A. *The Successful Christian School*. Pensacola, FL: A BEKA BOOK Publications, 1979.

Barton, David, C.L.I. Inc., P.O. Box 397, Aledo, TX 76008.

Bennis, Warren and Nanus, Burt. *Leaders: The Strategies For Taking Charge*. New York, NY: Harper & Row, 1985.

Billings, Robert J. *A Guide to the Christian School*. Washington, DC: Action Press, 1978.

Blumenfeld, Samuel L. *NEA: Trojan Horse In American Education*. Boise, ID: The Paradigm Co., 1984.

Brubaker, J. Lester. *Personnel Administration in the Christian School*. Winona Lake, IN: BMH, 1980.

Burkett, Larry. *Your Finances in Changing Times*. Chicago, IL: Moody Press, 1982.

Byrne, H.W. *A Christian Approach to Education*. Milford, MI: Mott Media, 1961.

Carter, Virginia L. and Garigan, Catherine S., Eds. *A Marketing Approach to Student Recruitment*. Washington, DC: Council for Advancement and Support of Education, 1979.

Churda, John B. "Athletics in the Christian School." James W. Deuink, Ed., *Some Light on Christian Education*. Greenville, SC: Bob Jones University Press, 1984.

Columbia Computing Service. 8611 South 212th St., Kent, WA 98031 (1-800-663-0544).

Conn, Harry. *Four Trojan Horses Of Humanism*. Milford, MI: Mott Media, 1982

Daugherty, Billy Joe. For a complete listing of sermons and tapes, write: Victory Books and Tapes, 7700 South Lewis Avenue, Tulsa, OK 74136.

Demuth, Dennis. "Christian School Education: No Longer An Option." DEL Publications, 5747 South Utica, Tulsa, OK 1983.

Demuth, Dennis. *Student Study and Assignment Guide*. Tulsa, OK: Victory Publications, 1982.

Demuth, Dennis; Black, Mary Martha; and Demuth, Carol. *GranDees: A School-Based Volunteer Program*. Tulsa, OK: Praise, Inc. 1990.

Demuth, Dennis, and Demuth, Carol. *Legal Requirements For Christian Schools*. Tulsa, OK: Praise, Inc. 1990.

Demuth, Dennis, and Demuth, Carol. *Spirit-Directed Discipline*. Tulsa, OK: DEL Publications (Work in progress).

Demuth, Dennis, and Demuth, Carol. *Spirit-Directed Model of Education*. Tulsa, OK: DEL Publications (Work in progress).

Deuink, James W. and Herbster, Carl D., *Effective Christian School Management*. Greenville, SC: Bob Jones University Press, 1986.

Deuink, James W., Ed. *Some Light On Christian Education*. Greenville, SC: Bob Jones University Press, 1984.

Deuink, James W. *The Ministry of the Christian School Guidance Counselor*. Greenville, SC: Bob Jones University Press, 1985.

Dill, Stephen P. "The Administration of the Development Program." Roy W. Lowrie, Jr., Ed. *Administration of The Christian School*. First Edition. Whittier, CA: The Association of Christian Schools International, 1984.

Dun and Bradstreet. "Collection Techniques." Business Education Services, 100 Church Street. New York, NY 10007, 1985.

Dura-Kote, Inc., P.O. Box 26309, Austin, TX 78755.

Elve, Philip. *Financing Christian Schools*. Grand Rapids, MI: Christian Schools International, 1984.

Ensman, Richard G., Jr. "Community Use of Your Facilities." in *Church Management: The Clergy Journal*. (March, 1991). pp.42,43.

Folks, John M. and Graham, Lloyd. *Bridges To Success*. Oklahoma City, OK: State Dept. of Education, 1984.

Gabler, Mel. "Educational Research Analysts." Longview, TX: The Mel Gablers, 1991.

Garrick, Gene. "Forward," Lowrie, Roy W., Jr. *To Those Who Teach in Christian Schools*. Whittier, CA: ACSI, 1978.

Goldstein, William and DeVita, Joseph C. *Successful School Communications: A Manual and Guide for Administrators*. West Nyack, NY: Parker Publishing Co., Inc. 1977.

Gospel Films, Inc., Post Office Box 455, Muskegon, MI 49443.

Hand, Catherine, and Sheth, Alice. "Guidelines for Library Collection," Tulsa, OK: Victory Christian School, 1989.

Hefley, James C. *Are Textbooks Harming Your Children*? Milford, MI: Mott Media 1979.

Hendrickson, Gayle A. *Promoting Continuing Education Programs*. Washington, DC: Council For Advancement and Support of Education, 1980.

Herr, Ethel. *Schools: How Parents Can Make A Difference*. Chicago, IL: Moody Press, 1981.

Hitchner, Kenneth W. and Hitchner, Anne Tifft. *Making A Difference In College Admission*. West Nyack, NY: The Center For Applied Research In Education, 1989.

Howard, Eugene R. *School Discipline Desk Book*. West Nyack, NY: Parker Publishing Co., Inc. 1978.

Hughes, Larry W. and Ubben, Gerald C. *The Elementary Principal's Handbook: A Guide to Effective Action*. Second Edition, Boston, MA: Allyon and Bacon, Inc., 1984.

If You Want Air Time. Washington, DC: National Association of Broadcasters, 1976.

International Christian Accrediting Association. *Elementary and Secondary Christian Schools: ICAA Official Visitors/Site Chairman's Manual*. Tulsa, OK: Oral Roberts University Educational Fellowship, 1987.

Jordan, K. Forbis; McKeown, Mary P.; Salmon, Richard G.; and Webb, Dean L. *School Business Administration*. Beverly Hills, CA: Sage Publications, Inc., 1985.

Kienel, Paul A. "Have You Enrolled Your Children In Christian Schools For The Right Reasons?" *Christian School Comment*. Whittier, CA: The Association of Christian Schools International, 1989.

Kienel, Paul A. *Reasons For Christian Schools*. Milford, MI: Mott Media, 1981.

Kienel, Paul A. *Reasons For Sending Your Child To A Christian School*. LaHabra, CA: P.K. Books, 1978.

Kienel, Paul A. "*Your Questions Answered About Christian Schools*." Whittier, CA: The Association of Christian Schools International, 1983.

Kienel, Paul A. *What This Country Needs*. San Diego, CA: Beta Books, 1977.

Krajewski, Robert J.; Martin, John S.; and Walden, John C. *The Elementary School Principalship*. New York, NY: Holt, Rinehart and Winston, 1983.

LaHaye, Tim. *The Battle for the Family*. Old Tappan, NJ: Fleming H. Revell Co., 1982.

"Let Their Eyes be Open." A 60-minute file produced by Regent University, Virginia Beach, VA 23464.

Lowrie, Roy W., Jr., Ed. *Administration of the Christian School*. Whittier, CA: The Association of Christian Schools International, 1984.

Lowrie, Roy W., Jr., Ed. *Evaluative Criteria For Christian Elementary School*. Wheaton, IL: National Association of Christian Schools, 1973.

Lowrie, Roy W., Jr. *Inside the Christian School: From The Headmaster's Diary*. Whittier, CA: Association of Christian Schools International, 1980.

Lowrie, Roy W., Jr. *To Those Who Teach in Christian Schools*. Whittier, CA: Association of Christian Schools International, 1978.

Macintosh, Neisha, and Demuth, Dennis. *Resource Center Handbook*. Tulsa, OK: Victory Publications, 1984.

Marks, James R., Stoops, Emery, and Stoops, Joyce King. *Handbook of Educational Supervision: A Guide For The Practitioner*. Boston, MA: Allyn and Bacon, Inc. 1971.

Mason, John L. *An Enemy Called Average*. Tulsa, OK: Harrison House, 1990.

McCrea, Bill. "To Accredit or Not?" *ORUEF Newsletter*, January 1991, 5.

Montapert, Alfred A. *The Supreme Philosophy of Man*. Englewood Cliffs, NJ: Prentice-Hall, Inc., 1970.

Moos, Rudolf H. and Trikett, Edison J. *Classroom Environment Scale*. Palo Alto, CA: Consulting Psychologists Press, Inc., 1974.

Norris, Murray. *Weep For Your Children*. Christian Family Renewal, Box 73, Clovis, CA 93613 (209-291-4958).

Parkhurst, William. *How To Get Publicity: And Make The Most Of It Once You've Got It*. New York, NY: Times Books, 1985.

Peters, Thomas J. and Waterman, Robert H., Jr. *In Search Of Excellence*. New York, NY: Warner Books, 1982.

Peters, Tom and Austin, Nancy. *A Passion for Excellence*. New York, NY: Warner Books, Inc. 1985.

Petry, Don D. *Elementary and Secondary Christian Schools Standards and Procedures Manual*. The International Christian Accrediting Association, 7777 South Lewis Avenue, Tulsa, OK 74171, 1989.

Prentice, Albert. *Modern Custodian*. Fourth Edition. Orlando, FL: Institutional Management Services, 1968.

Roberts, Oral. *Miracles of Seed Faith*. Revised edition. Tulsa, OK: Oral Roberts Evangelistic Association, 1982.

Roth, David L. "Public Relations." Roy W. Lowrie Jr., Ed., *Administration of the Christian School*. Whittier, CA: ACSI, 1984.

Ruddick Research International, Inc. "Parent Climate Study For Victory Christian School." Tulsa, OK: 1984.

Rush, Myron. *Management: A Biblical Approach*. Wheaton, IL: Victor Books, 1983.

Sanders, Oswald, J. *Spiritual Leadership*. Chicago, IL: The Moody Press, 1980.

Schindler, Claude E., Jr., and Pacheco, Pyle. *Educating for Eternity*. Whittier, CA: Association of Christian Schools International, 1979.

Schindler, Claude E., Jr., Pacheco, Pyle, and Karnehm, Steve. *The Role of Athletics in the Christian School*. Whittier, CA: ACSI, 1981.

Schindler, Claude E., Jr. *Sowing for Excellence*. Whittier, CA: Association of Christian Schools International, 1987.

Seville Classics, Inc. 251 Redondo Beach Blvd., Gardena, CA 90248 (1-213-538-2340).

Skillbank II. 15 Governors Court, Baltimore, MY 211207, 1988. Phone 1-800-451-5726.

Steensma, Geraldine J. and Van Brummelen, Harro W., Eds. *Shaping School Curriculum: A Biblical View*. Terre Haute, IN: Signal, 1977.

Stern, Gary J. *Marketing Workbook For Non-Profit Organizations*. St. Paul, MN: Amherst H. Wilder Foundation, 1990.

"Taking Liberties: The Legacy of the ACLU." Coral Ridge Ministries. P.O. Box 407132, Fort Lauderdale, FL 33340, 1991 (1-800-229-9673).

The American College Testing Program. *Study Power*. 250 Wireless Boulevard, Hauppauge, NY 11788, 1987.

"The Capsule." Caravans For Christ, Inc. 1205 West Fifth St., Cameron, MO 64429, 1991.

The Proper Use of Standardized Tests: Subjective Testing and Grading. Greenville, SC: Bob Jones University Press, 1986.

Classroom Testing. Greenville, SC: Bob Jones University Press, 1986.

Tidwell, Charles A. *Church Administration Effective Leadership for Ministry*. Nashville, TN: Broadman Press, 1985.

Wade, Theodore E., Jr. and Others. *The Home School Manual*. Fourth Edition. Auburn, CA: Gazelle Publications, 1991.

Wagner, C. Peter. *Strategies For Church Growth*. Ventura, CA: Regal Books, 1987.

Ward, David. *Zoe Health Fitness*. Tulsa, OK: Victory Christian School, 7700 South Lewis Avenue, Tulsa, OK, 1983.

What Works: Research About Teaching and Learning. Washington DC: U.S. Department of Education, 1986.

White, Raymond E., and Enderlin, August C., eds. *Manual of Administration for Christian Schools*. First Edition. Whittier, CA: The Association of Christian Schools International, 1986.

Yarrington, Roger. *Community Relations Handbook*. New York, NY: Longman, Inc., 1983.

Appendix A

Senior Pastor Discount

(Date)

(Senior Pastor)
(Name of Church)
(Address)
(City, State zip)

Dear (Name of Pastor):

This letter is to inform you of Pastor (Sponsoring Church pastor, Headmaster, etc.) desire to allow more children from churches with similar foundational principles and vision to be part of (Name of Christian school). With this in view, we are providing an opportunity for children of the Senior Pastor to attend (Name of Christian School) at a special discount rate (44 percent of the non-member rate, or whatever rate is established).

In addition, it is our desire to offer to each church a special Church Sponsorship Program. Children from your ministry would be permitted to attend (Name of School) at the same tuition rate (44% of the non-member rate), if your church would pay the remaining portion of tuition - much like the sponsoring Church does for its members. Participation in this program would allow your church to offer to your members a quality Christian education without having the expense of establishing and maintaining an entire K-12th grade school system.

Several churches are already participating in these Sponsorship Programs. Some have added a tuition assistance program to their budget, others have reserved funds from their outreach giving, while others have presented the need to members of the congregation and received offerings for a general scholarship fund.

Enclosed is an instructional packet, as well as samples of our enrollment packet.

If you have any further questions, please call 918-493-1700.

In His Service,

Superintendent

Senior Pastor Discount

1.Complete the enclosed application. Forward the application to (Name of School), attention: Church Sponsorship Program.
2.Since participation in this program is by invitation only, a confirming letter will be sent to the Senior Pastor.
3.This confirming letter will be presented at the time student enrollment applications are submitted to the school office. All students must meet enrollment standards and requirements.

Application for Senior Pastor Discount

Name of Church: ____
Address: ____
City:________________________State:______Zip:_____Phone:_________
Name of Senior Pastor: _____________________________________
Number of years as senior pastor: ______________________________
Names of Senior Pastor's Children participating in Senior Pastor Program and grade

____
____
____

Each student must meet VCS enrollment and admission standards and complete an official VCS enrollment application.

This discount does not include enrollment fees, or other fees; e.g., books, sports participation, driver's education, etc., which must be paid at time of enrollment.

Signature of Senior Pastor___________________________Date_____________

Church Sponsorship Program

1. You would establish criteria for selection of recipients. You may wish to identify priority categories, such as widows, missionaries, those in full-time ministry, truly fatherless, single parents, etc. You may select those students who have expressed an interest in going into the ministry. (Please note that IRS does not approve of tuition assistance or scholarship programs that require parents to make any minimal donation to a church in order to qualify for such a program. Any such required donations would be disallowed as a deduction by an IRS agent in the event that the taxpayer were audited.)
2. In order to be accepted at (Name of Christian School), students must meet all enrollment and admission standards/requirements.
3. You would identify the number of children to be sponsored.
4. Create a sponsorship application (see enclosure).
5. Appoint a Sponsorship Review Board.
6. Families who qualify would complete the application and be interviewed by the Sponsorship Review Board.

7. If approved, the parents will sign an agreement letter. A copy is given to the parent and a copy is sent to the school. The copy must be received before a parent can proceed with the enrollment process.
8. A list of sponsorship students who have enrolled will be forwarded to the church.
9. Sponsorship payments are made in one of the following ways: a) Yearly (paid on or before Aug. 26th); b) By the semester (paid on or before Aug. 26th., and Jan. 6th.)

These payments must be made on time in order for the sponsored students to remain enrolled at (Name of School). Parents will be required to stay current with their portion of tuition payments. Should a parent have to withdraw prior to the conclusion of the semester or end of year, the unused portion sponsored by the church will be refunded or applied to sponsor other children at your option.

Church Sponsorship Agreement

This agreement is between ______________________________ (Name of Church) and ______________________________(Name of Christian School) for (School Term).
Believing that a quality Christian education is important to Christian families and to our church, we agree to sponsor the children of:

____
(Parent's Name)

Names of Children	Grade	Non-member Tuition

The total annual tuition is ______________________________
The parents (guardian) will pay ______________________________
Church payments will be made by the ______________________________
(By semester on or before Aug. 26th, and Jan. 6th, or yearly paid by Aug. 26th.)

It is further understood that this payment is for tuition only and does not apply toward enrollment fees, books, or other activity fees for the school year which are to be paid by the family.
This agreement is dated ______________________________

____
Church Representative Title Date

____
Parent (Guardian) Father

____
Parent (Guardian) Mother

Appendix B

Christian Radio Announcements

Over the next few weeks, KCFO will help answer the question, "Why I haven't put my children in a Christian School?"

Excuse Number 1:

"I'm not sure of the philosophy of Christian school education."

RESPONSE:

"God gave us a commandment to train up a child in the way he should go so that later in life he will have a strong foundation to hang on to and build on. The purpose of Christian school education is to help parents to do just that, to present to our children the truth about God, about life and living, about our world and everything in it and to present the Word of God as the authoritative source upon which to build a life that has purpose and meaning.

It's an educational process that puts the Bible at the center and asks the student and the teacher to evaluate all they see in the world through the eyes of God, because God is truth. All must conform to Him or it is not truth...Jesus said, "I am the way, the truth, and the life." In true Christian education, students learn to use the Bible to evaluate all of life. The Bible is life - it is the Living Word - it is above every other book.

There are several quality Christian schools in the area. Call one for an appointment today to see what they can do for your children and their future."

Excuse Number 2:

"Aren't Christian schools merely private schools for the rich?"

RESPONSE:

"The answer is no. There's a big difference between private schools and Christian schools. Christian schools are private schools only in the sense that they are not funded by the government.

Many private schools are often as secular as public schools. Most of them are quality academic institutions, but they do not have a Christian purpose. So, in reality, there are three distinct types of schools - public, private, and religious. Public and private schools have a different funding base but the same basic secular humanistic philosophy. Private and religious schools have the same funding base, tuition, but a different philosophy - man-centered education vs. God-centered education.

Parents should be vitally concerned about the educational philosophy of the school their children attend. It is one thing to prepare students to make a living; it is quite another to train them how to live.

Inspiring students to live a life totally surrendered to Jesus Christ is the ultimate goal of Christian school educators.

Private school educators have a secular educational objective for their students. They lack a Christian point of view and they are often as secular as the public schools. There are several quality Christian schools in the area. Call one for an appointment today to see what they can do for your children and their future."

Appendix C

Answers to Questions Most Frequently Asked

ACADEMICS. How do students rank academically?

Students at Victory, over the past nine years, have scored on an average, no less than one and one half years above national norms. Since the first graduating class, high school SAT and ACT test scores have averaged above the national norm with most students qualifying for academic scholarships. Since 1987, Victory has produced 2 National Merit Scholars, 4 semi-finalists and 3 commended students. The average G.P.A. is 3.1 on a scale of 4.0.

ACCREDITATION. Is the school accredited?

Victory is recognized by two accrediting agencies. First of all, since 1983, Victory has been accredited by the International Christian Accrediting Association. Secondly, Victory has been recommended for accreditation with the State of Oklahoma Department of Education. Parents provide the final test of accreditation. If a school is doing a good job, it will continue to grow. Over past five years, Victory has averaged over 700 students in grades K - 12th. It started in 1979 with only 226 students.

BIBLE. Do the students have Bible classes?

All elementary students have Bible daily. The curriculum is from Radiant Press. This curriculum includes Bible memory work. Chapels are presented weekly. At the secondary level, students attend Bible class three days per week; one day is spent in Chapel and one day in Bible seminar. All 9th and 10th grade students are required to take a course in New and Old Testament survey. Upper-level Bible classes are geared to the needs of the student. Courses have included: 1) Christian Financial Concepts, 2) Strategic Planning for Your Life, 3) Practical Christian Living, 4) Prayer, Missions, Evangelism, 5) Names of God, Gifts of The Spirit, Fruits of The Spirit, etc.

A special music ministry class is available for those who have a special gift for music. Also, a missions class may be selected by those students interested in ministry and missions. Both special classes have opportunity to participate in ministry outreaches to the community, state and nations. In the past, students have gone to: Costa Rica, Mexico, Jamaica, Guatemala, Belize and England. They have participated in: Street Ministry, Preaching, Music, Youth Group Training, Physical Labor, Drama and Counseling.

CERTIFICATION. Are all teachers certified?

All teachers are required to hold a degree in their area of expertise, as well as holding an Oklahoma teaching certificate for the subjects they teach. In addition, Victory Christian School believes that the type of training and range of experience, coupled with the lifestyle of the teacher, are important predictors of teaching success. It is our goal to have the best teachers possible. Presently, Victory Christian School teaching staff has an average of 12 years of experience.

COLLEGE. What percentage of your students go on to college?

Approximately 87 percent of the students go on to post high school study. Since 1981, Victory has graduated 481 students. Post high school studies have included: University of Arkansas, Arizona State University, California State College, Catawba College, University of Colorado, Delrango College, Evangel College, Friends University, Furman University, Georgetown University, John Brown University, Judson College, Kansas Newman College, Mary Washington College, University of Miami, University of Missouri, North Central Bible College, Northeastern State University, Bacone College, Oklahoma State University, University of Oklahoma, Oral Roberts University, Penn State University, St. Johns University, Taylor University, Texas Women's College, University of Tulsa, Wayne State University, Wheaton College, William Jewell College, University of Wisconsin, Central Piedmont Community College, Christ For The Nations, Community College of Maryland, Hudson Community College, Oklahoma Junior College, Ottawa College, Rhema, Rogers State College, Cosmetology School, ITT Technical Institute, Pipe Trades School, Spartan, Army, Marines, National Guard and Navy.

COMPUTERS. Are there computers in all the classrooms?

Victory has a new $60,000 computer lab with 26 state-of-the-art work stations. In addition, student grades 4-6 have access to computers in the classroom. A computer literacy program is provided for students, grades K5-12th. All students are required to pass a computer literacy test in order to graduate.

COURSES. What courses can students take?

Victory offers traditional self-contained classes for grades K4-6th. Presently, there are two to three classrooms at each grade level. The junior high and high school programs contain a variety of courses that are typically offered at these levels. In addition, Victory provides accelerated, as well as honor courses. Special labs in Math and English are available for students who need extra assistance. It is our goal that all students who graduate will be prepared to enter college. Both elementary and secondary students have fine arts courses; vocal music, instrumental music, art, drama and speech.

CURRICULUM. What kind of curriculum do you use?

It is our goal to use curricula that help meet the educational needs of our students. Presently in the elementary level, we use materials from the following companies: A-Beka - History/Social Studies, Bob Jones - Reading, York - K4-4th, Merrill - Spelling, Houton Mifflin - Language, Saxon - Math.

Publishers at the secondary level include: A-Beka - English/Social Studies, Bob Jones - Science, South Western - Business, Saxon - Math.

FACILITIES. What about your facilities?

The school is housed in a new facility. The classrooms are modern with new labs for the sciences and a complete computer lab. Computer literacy is taught at early ages of elementary. Specialty rooms for art, vocal music and instrumental music with teachers specially trained to teach these subjects.

Functional activity center that houses four gym floors, an indoor running track, aerobic area, cafeteria, and space for assemblies and meetings. There is also a large modern library.

FINE ART. Does Victory offer Fine Arts classes?

Victory provides several opportunities for students to express God given talents and abilities. These include: Drama, Senior directed one act plays - major productions - "The Hiding Place," "The Miracle Worker," "Best Christmas Pageant Ever," "Cheaper By The Dozen," "The Sound of Music."

VCS has produced a Musical/Comedy and taken it to England. The school is involved in Speech Competition - currently ranked fifth in the state in Speech. We have had state winners in drama, speech and debate.

SPORTS. What grade levels can participate in sports?

Victory has over 40 sport teams with competition at all levels. Activities include: Cheerleading, Volleyball, Basketball, Track, Soccer, Cross-Country, Baseball, Tennis, Softball and Golf. In the past ten years, students at Victory have achieved a total of eight national Christian school championships in cheerleading, soccer and basketball, and two state volleyball championships.

Students have received sport scholarships at: Oral Roberts University, Evangel College, Friends University, Ottawa College, Bartlesville Wesleyan, Bacone, Judson College, Eastern College.

STUDENT-TEACHER RATIO. What is the teacher-pupil ratio?

Over the past ten years, Victory's teacher-pupil ratio has averaged 1:23 for all grade levels. Our class sizes are limited to a maximum of 28 students at the elementary level. This year, the elementary school averaged 1:22. At the high school level, we have courses with as few as 7 students and as high as 35 in some popular upper-division classes; e.g., Senior English. Secondary classes averaged 1:24 this past year. When we include our counseling and administrative staff, those who have a great influence upon the lives of our students, Victory's student to staff ratio is 1:18.

TUITION ASSISTANCE. How do I apply for tuition assistance?

In our attempt to see as many students attend Victory as possible, discounts have been provided for payment by the year or semester. Discounts are given for more than one child attending school. Payments can be made over 9 to 12 months. Families with special financial needs can also apply for additional assistance in the form of a work study. These applications are available in the school office after May 1st.

Victory also offers free books and no re-enrollment fees for continuing students who re-enroll during our special re-enrollment discount period. This constitutes a savings of $150.00 to $290.00 each year. Many of our families have saved hundreds of dollars.

UNIFORMS. Do you wear uniforms?

Victory has a standardized dress code. The uniforms provide for great variety in combinations of red, navy, blue, white, grey, yellow, khaki and plaid. Sweaters include v-neck, vest or cardigans in navy, grey and red. Our parents and students have been very satisfied with Victory's uniforms.

Appendix D

Alumni Census

Please help us update our records and gather valuable information. Please respond to as many questions as possible. Please enclose a recent photograph.

PERSONAL

Name:____ Phone:________

Address:____

State:____________________________________ Zip Code: __________

Marital Status: Married _________________ Single _________________

Children: Number and ages ____________________________________

High school grade point average:_______________________________

Year graduated: _________________ ____________________________

Employment: Full time _____ Part time ________

Business employed by:/Position

____

CHURCH INFORMATION

Name of church presently attending:

____

Senior pastor:

____

Are you involved in a leadership position? No____ Yes _____,

Please identify the position:__________________________________

Are you involved in the five-fold areas of ministry? No_______ Yes _____

Please check: Pastor___ Evangelist ___ Teacher ___ Prophet ___ Apostle____

Did you participate in a missions trip while at Victory? Yes___ No ___

Please identify trip and year:_________________________________

Have you been involved in missions since graduating? Yes/No____________

Please explain nature of involvement:

____

____

ADDITIONAL EDUCATION

Name(s) of schools attended: Include names and dates attended

____

____

Graduated:yes or no ___________ Plan to graduate: Date ______________

Planned occupation:

____

Major: ______________ Minor: _____________

Grade point average: ___________________________

Most difficult course:

___

Least difficult course:

___

Approximate cost per semester:
Tuition _______ fees _____ housing_____ transportation _____ personal needs _______
Financial aid received: Yes/No______ Kind: ______________________

INFORMATION FEEDBACK

1. Which course(s) (other than art, music and physical education) at Victory were the easiest for you?

___

2. Which course(s) at Victory were the most difficult?

___

3. Which course(s) at Victory best prepared you for the direction you are headed?

___

4. If you could change any aspect of VCS, what would that be and why?

___

5. What words of encouragement would you give students concerning the spiritual lifestyle needed to be successful after graduation?

___

___

6. What words of encouragement would you give students who would like to skip college?

___

7. What have been the greatest spiritual challenges you have faced since graduation?

___

Post High School Education

1. Did you have any challenges being accepted at a college or technical school? Yes/No____ Please explain:______________________________

___

2. Which upper division course(s) were adequate in preparing you for college?

___

3. How can we improve those courses that were not effective in preparing you for college?

___

4. What could our counselors have done to help you better plan for college?

___

5. What can VCS do to better inform students of college choices?

___

6. How can VCS better communicate to parents the need for college?

___

7. What words of advice would you give parents of students preparing for college?

___

8. What one thing about college do you enjoy best?

---

9. Other than academically, what would you like to tell juniors and seniors on "how to plan for college"?

---

10. How would you respond to the statement "college is a process of growth"?

Involvement

1. Would you be willing to speak to VCS students to encourage them in better preparing for their future?

---

2. Would you be willing to help in establishing an alumni association?

---

3. Please place a check next to the area of interest you would like to be involved in:

_____officer: pres., v/p, secretary, treasurer, chaplain,
_____newsletter - follow-up mailings to alumni,
_____alumni directory,
_____planning and preparing for activities such as: annual alumni game, homecoming, class reunions, graduations.

*** If you have had a special miracle or testimony, please share it with us ***

Appendix E

Parent Questionnaire

The Parent Action Team would appreciate your help in completing this questionnaire. Its purpose is to promote communication between VCS administrators, parents and students. We desire to keep our spiritual, academic and extracurricular programs strong and to improve in areas where needed.

Please fill out the questionnaire individually (except married couples) and return it to the PAT box in the school office by February 28, 1992. We will publish the results when we are finished. Thank you for your help and prayers.

1. My child's grade is:
   K4/K5________
   1 - 6 _________
   7 - 8 _________
   9 - 12 ________
2. My child(ren) have been in VCS for ____ years.
3. In general, I am (check below) with the education at VCS.
   _____ Very Pleased ____ Somewhat Pleased
   _____Fairly Pleased _____ Unhappy Upset _______
4. My child(ren) plan to (check below) return to VCS next year:
   _____Definitely _______ Definitely Not
   _____Possibly ________ Definitely Not Due to Graduation
5. Are you a member of Victory Christian Center? _______YES______NO
6. Please rate the following areas:
   Rating Scale: 1 = Poor, 2 = Below Average, 3 = Average, 4 = Excellent, 5 = Outstanding, Leave blank for no opinion.
   _____________Academics
   _____________Discipline
   _____________Spiritual
   _____________Boy's Sports
   _____________Girl's Sports
   _____________Cheerleading
   _____________Drama
   _____________Choir
   _____________Band
   _____________Homework (amount, difficulty, etc.)
   _____________Other (Please Specify): ______________

Please answer the following questions in your own words; be as complete as possible (Print or Type).

7. How do you feel about the dress code?

____

How, if anything, might the dress code be improved?

8. How do you feel about discipline at VCS?

Grades 7-12 - If your son/daughter is in grades 7-12:

9. What is their favorite subject and why? (Please discuss this with your child. You may select more than one subject if you desire.)

10. Who is their favorite teacher and why?

11. What clubs do you/your children participate in?

12. What clubs that are not currently at VCS would you like to see started?

13. Would you like to have a Science Booster Club started?

14. Would you participate?

15. Would you like to volunteer to help in any areas at VCS? (If so, please indicate area and then contact the office.)

16. What are the strengths of Victory Christian School?

17. What are the weaknesses of Victory Christian School?

18. How might they be IMPROVED?

19. Please comment on any other aspects of Victory Christian School that you wish to address:

Appendix F

New Student Information

Name: ____

Date of Birth: ______________________ Grade: ____________________

Transfer from: ____

Brothers and Sisters:

Name Grade

____

____

____

____

When and where were you saved?

____

____

Which church do you attend?

____

____

What subjects do you like best?

____

____

What subjects do you have to work hardest at?

____

____

What sports do you play?

____

____

Artistic and music ability?

____

Other talents or abilities?

____

____

What were your last semester's grades?

Math: _____ English: _____ History: _____ Science: _____

Bible: _____ Other: ____________________________

____

Other helpful information: ____________________________

____

____

Appendix G

Field Trip Evaluation

Activity:____

Date of Activity: ____

Person making this evaluation

____

Role of person in activity:

____

Original objective:

____

What were the high points of the activity?

____

What were the low points of the activity?

____

____

____

____

____

____

Rate each of the following

1 =Not nearly enough
2 =Barely enough
3 =Sufficient
4 =More than enough

________Preparation
________Transportation
________Supervision
________Arrangements (lodging, food, etc)
________Discipline by students
________Leadership of person in charge

What would you have changed about this activity to improve its effectiveness?

____

____

I would____

______ highly recommend this activity
______recommend this activity
______not recommend this activity

NOTE: Attach the original activity request approval to this evaluation.

Appendix H

Book Screening

Books selected for the library must be consistent with the library statement of philosophy. For example, the library is established to (See Victory Christian School, Guidelines for Library Collection, 1989):

1. Support and compliment the courses taught in the school's curriculum and to aid in the improvement of reading skills.
2. Extend and diversify the opportunities available for the student's spiritual and intellectual growth.
3. Provide opportunities for quality Christian recreational reading.
4. Enable the student to become aware of the resources available to Christians as aids to Christian witness and service.
5. Introduce the student to the rich heritage of edifying literature from other ages and cultures, Christian and otherwise.
6. Develop an appreciation for fine literature.
7. Provide resource material for the teaching faculty, members of the school community and of the ministry.

The purpose of the Christian School library is:

1. Provide guidance and advice to the user in a caring, Christian atmosphere.
2. Exercise spiritual and moral discernment in the selection, arrangement, display and availability of materials.
3. Provide a suitable range of materials to fulfill the purposes stated above.
4. Seek to match materials to the level of spiritual and intellectual development of the users.
5. Endeavor to provide maximum security for its resources; at the same time, provide the simplest and easiest circulation procedures to facilitate maximum use of its resources.

The Victory Christian School library uses the following guidelines for selection of textbooks, teaching materials and library books which:

1. Are impartial in content and interpretations, and do not encourage or condone civil disorder, social strife, or disregard for the law.

2. Do not lower and high moral standards of honesty, respect for parents, teachers, and those in authority, the existence of absolute standards of God.

3. Do not degrade the family as the core of American society, nor the roles of men and women, boys and girls.

4. Foster free enterprise.

5. Place religion as a significant influence upon the course of history and the affairs of man.

6. Present a well-balanced and factual approach to controversial, political and social movements without biased editorial judgments.

7. Do not promote illegal lifestyles or sexual behavior, sadistic or degrading behavior.

8. Do not include blatantly offensive language or illustrations.

9. Do not include violence for reasons of excitement, sensationalism, or as an excuse for relevance. Violence, if it appears in textbook content, shall be treated in context of cause and consequences.

10. Treat the subject of historical origins of humankind in an objective and unbiased manner.

11. Do not invade the privacy of the pupils or pupils' parents.

Appendix I

Guidance Program Checkup

It is our desire to improve our guidance services. In order to do this, we need your assistance. Your honest response to the following survey will help us better plan so the school can be of greater value to students who enroll. Indicate your response by marking **X** in the appropriate space. Answer YES or NO if possible.

Yes No

___ ___ 1. Did your high school course fit your interests?
___ ___ 2. Were your courses adapted to your abilities?
___ ___ 3. Did they meet your needs?
___ ___ 4. Did you obtain an estimate of your scholastic ability?
___ ___ 5. Were you informed of your scholastic ability?
___ ___ 6. Were you informed of the results of achievement tests?
___ ___ 7. Were you informed of the results of standardized aptitude and interest tests?
___ ___ 8. Was there sufficient opportunity to obtain individual counseling?
___ ___ 9. Did you receive assistance in planning your vocational career after graduation?
___ ___ 10. Did you receive assistance in planning your school program?
___ ___ 11. If you planned to go on to college after graduation, did you receive assistance in planning to meet your college entrance requirements?
___ ___ 12. Did you receive a personal interview from an administrator as part of the enrollment process?
___ ___ 13. Did you receive any instruction on effective study skills?
___ ___ 14. Have you made new friends since being at this school?
___ ___ 15. If you are going to college, do you have an idea of your major area of study?

Please indicate the extent of assistance received while in this high school from the school personnel: teachers, counselors, principal, etc.

Place the letter of the word that best describes the amount of assistance received in front of each statement

N = None, L = Little, A = Average, AA = Above Average and M = Much.

_____1. Planning my high school program to fit my interests.
_____2. Reviewing and evaluating my accumulative record.
_____3. Evaluating my achievement test results.
_____4. Making a comprehensive self-appraisal.
_____5. Planning my high school program to fit my needs and abilities.

_____6. Reviewing and developing my personality.
_____7. Overcoming personal handicaps, such as shyness, impoliteness.
_____8. Evaluating my scores on aptitude tests.
_____9. Evaluating my scores on interest inventories and personality tests.
____10. Becoming informed of the educational opportunities in high school.
____11. Developing spiritually.
____12. The selection of my high school courses.
____13. Accumulating information concerning after graduation.
____14. Becoming informed of vocational opportunities and requirements.
____15. Planning my future.
____16. Getting adjusted to high school.
____17. Solving the problems concerning social life.
____18. Solving problems relating to my emotional behavior.
____19. Taking the best advantage of the social life of the community for my own welfare.
____20. Overcoming mistakes.
____21. Developing a well-balanced, poised and cultured personality.
____22. Receiving helpful suggestions in developing desirable conduct.
____23. My participation in school activities.
____24. Stimulating my interests in spiritual concerns.
____25. Setting up goals within my own abilities.
____26. Developing effective study habits.
___ 27. Integrating Biblical principles into my decision-making processes.
___28. Listening to the voice of the Spirit of God.

Appendix J

Cleaning Tasks

Items	D	W	M	A N
Empty waste paper baskets and wipe them off inside and out with a cloth.	X			
Empty pencil sharpener. Oil twice a year.	X			
Clean chalk boards and chalk rails, unless notified to save.	X			
Clean floors.	X			
Dust all areas where dust will collect, including desks, shelves, tops of cupboards, windows sash and blinds, molding, mop boards and doors.	X			
Clean sink and sink tops.	X			
Clean finger marks from windows.		X		
Wash windows.				X
Keep pencil marks washed off desks, backs of chairs and around pencil sharpener.	X			
Clear tops of desks and tables.	X			
Replace burned light bulbs.				X
Clean restrooms, toilets, urinals, sinks, mirrors.	X			
Check and fill soap dispensers.	X			
Check and fill paper dispensers.	X			
Clean restroom walls.				X
Wet mop toilet rooms, tile, concrete and terrazzo.	X			

Items	D	W	M	A N
Clean shower rooms.	X			
Collect trash from rooms and place in central location.	X			
Check science room for safety.	X			
Check playground equipment.			X	
Treat gym floor.				X
Maintain grounds and landscaping				X
Cafeteria equipment inspection - mixers, peelers, dishwashers, fans, exhaust, knives, chopper, etc.			X	
Refrigerator motors - clean every 6 months, fill oil cups every 6 months.			X	
Electrical switches - every two months, broken plates, spring switch, exposed fixtures or wiring.			X	
Down spouts, eaves, drains. Clean thoroughly. Check roof for leaks or damage.			X	
Doors and windows. Oil hinges every two months. Seal doors once a year, top and bottom.				X
Grease traps.			X	
Boilers. Dry run in August. Check all gauges.				X
Stage equipment. Check rollers, worn ropes, electrical, etc.			X	
Vehicles. Daily pre-trip inspections. Yearly inspection of all operating systems. Lubricate every 3000 miles or four months, whichever is sooner.	X			
Fire extinguishers - hose and pressure. Continually check for vandalism.			X	
AV equipment.			X	
Water fountains. Check for leaks twice a month.			X	

D = Daily
W = Weekly
M = Monthly
AN = As Needed

Appendix K

Tuition Assistance Application

Victory Christian School (VCS) is a ministry of Victory Christian Center (VCC). Applicants for financial aid must meet the following basic requirement in order for their application to be considered: Parents consider Victory Christian Center their home church and have established a history of regular attendance to Victory Christian Center.

Since it is not possible to provide aid to all who apply, VCS has established several priority categories for assistance. Listed from highest to lowest, these categories include:

1. Widows
2. Families whose parents/guardians are involved in overseas missionary outreaches on a full-time basis.
3. Families currently involved in full-time ministry.
4. Truly fatherless (father has deserted the family and no contact has been made and no financial support is available).
5. Single parent families.

Financial aid is awarded according to the merits of each applicant, monies available, class placement and category priorities. Parents will be informed in writing as to whether or not aid has been granted. Aid generally covers only part of the tuition costs. Parents are responsible for all remaining tuition and fees. Failure to meet this financial responsibility will result in aid being discontinued. Students who receive aid must remain in good standing academically, behaviorally and spiritually in order for the aid to continue. Aid is not automatic from year to year and must be applied for each year. No assurances are given that approval will be granted for the next year.

Your tuition aid application must be accompanied by a completed student application and a copy of your previous two years' income tax returns.

Applications for aid will be accepted no earlier than two months before the start of the school term and no later than one week before the start of the school term. Information submitted with the application will be considered confidential and reviewed only by those serving on the Financial Aid Committee. Falsification of any information will disqualify the applicant for financial aid. Should your financial status change during the period of time that the aid is in effect, you are required to contact the school office. All recipients of financial aid must attend Victory Christian Center's Financial Planning Class or Seminar.

This application must be received by the School office no later than August 10 for priority consideration. To avoid delay in processing, all items must be complete.

Date: ________________
Parent of Guardian: ____
Last Name First Name
Address:____
City: ____________________________ State: ____________ Zip: __________
Home Phone: ____

Student Information - Oldest to Youngest

Last Name	First Name	Middle	Birthdate	Grade

Church Information
How many services do you attend at Victory per month? ______________________
What leadership positions are you or have you held? ______________________
Date first attended Victory? ______________ Are you a member? ____________
Date converted: ____________ Date of Water Baptism: ____________

Financial Aid Classification (Please check ONE)
__ Widow __ Overseas Missionary __ Full-time Ministry __ Truely Fatherless
__ Single Parent
Please explain why you quality for this classification:______________________
____
____
____

EMPLOYMENT INFOMATION
Mother's Place of Employment: ______________________________________
Address:____
Position:_________________________________ Pnone:_________________
Social Security Number:____
How long have you been with this employer? _________________________
Previous employer: ___________________________ Length of Time: __________

Father's Place of Employment: ______________________________________
Address:____
Position:_________________________________ Pnone:_________________
Social Security Number:____
How long have you been with this employer? _________________________
Previous employer: ___________________________ **Length of Time:** __________

FINANCIAL INFORMATION

Property and Insurance

Assets	What is it worth now?	What is owed on it?
Home (Renters enter "O")		
Business and Farm		
Other Real Estate		
Investments		
Life Insurance		

Cash and Savings Accounts

Type of Account	Amount
Checking	
Savings	
CDs	
IRA	
Cash on hand	
Other	

Do you own _____ or rent _____ a house _____ or apartment? _____
Make of Auto: _______________ Year? ______ Value? ____________
Have you ever received financial assistance or any kind? ____ Yes ____ No
If "Yes", please explain:______________________________________

____

What other cources of income have your tried? ____________________

____

Joint Estimated **Monthly** Income

Item	Amount
Wages, Salaries, Tips, etc.	
Interest Income	
Dividents	
Other Income; business, rents, pensions, trusts, etc.	
Total Income	

Estimated Monthly Expenses

Item	Cost $	Other Expenses	Cost $
Tuition and Fees			
Rent/Mortage			
Utilities			
Food			
Medical			
Auto			
Insurance			
Column Total		**Grand Total**	

List other financial obligations which affect your need for assistance.

Creditor	Purpose	Due Date	Amount

Do you have a yearly/monthly budget? ____ Yes ____ No

STATEMENT OF YOUR NEED FOR FINANCIAL AID: Give any unusual circumstances affecting the financial status of your family that would help us to assess your request for financial assistance for the coming year.

____

____

____

____

____

____

____

____

____

____

____

What is the **minimum** amount of monthly aid needed? ______________

Please indicate the reasons why you feel a Christian education is important.

____
____
____
____
____
____
____
____
____
____
____
____
____
____
____
____
____
____
____
____
____
____
____
____
____
____

I certify that all of the preceding information is accurate.

Signature of Father or Guardian: ______________________________ Date:_____

Signature of Mother or Guardian: ______________________________ Date:_____

Appendix L

New Student Reward

Please take this opportunity to be informed of an exciting new student promotional. It is called the "New Student Reward." It could save you hundreds of dollars on next year's tuition. The procedures are as follows:

1. You must be a parent with at least one student currently enrolled at school.
2. For each new student who you are personally responsible for enrolling, you will receive $100 off your next year's total tuition.
3. New students are those who have not attended in the past 12 months.
4. The new parent must turn in the "New Student Reward" form. Only one family can receive credit for each new student.
5. The enlisting parent will receive the $100 per student after the newly enlisted student has completed two months in school and has a current tuition balance. Enlisting parents will receive tuition credit rather than cash.
6. There is no limit to the number of new students you can enroll for credit. Tuition credit can be carried over to the next year.

New Student Reward Certification

I, ____

(Printed Name of Parent of New Student)

hereby certify that the person named below was chiefly responsible for me enrolling my child(ren) in Victory Christian School. He/She personally initiated contact with me for the purpose of encouraging me to enroll my child(ren) in Victory Christian School. My children have not been previously enrolled in the past 12 months.

I have enrolled the following student(s):

Student's Name Grade

____

____

____

____

The person who encouraged me to enroll my child (ren) was:

Name ____

Address ____

City, State and Zip ____

Phone ____

Certified by ____

(Signature of Enrolling Parent Date

Appendix M

Before and After School Supervision
Grades 2 - 6

Dear Victory Parents:

We are providing a before and after school activities program for students from grade 2 through grade 6. The program will meet every day from 7:00 A.M. to 8:00 A.M. and from 3:00 P.M. to 5:30 P.M.

You may enroll your son/daughter in this program by completing an enrollment form, an emergency care authorization form and paying a $10.00 registration fee. You must then purchase an activities ticket. If you purchase 1 to 5 hours, your cost is $2.00 per hour. Six through 30 hours cost $1.50 per hour. A monthly ticket costs $1.25 per hour. Your ticket will be punched in half-hour segments as it is used.

Meeting Location

We will meet in Room 210 on the 2nd floor at 7:00 a.m. and no later than 3:08 p.m. Students arriving after 7:00 a.m. in the morning are to report directly to Room 210. If the group is not there, a note will be left on the door telling where the group may be found.

Activity Areas

Our activities will take place in the activities center, aerobics center, Room 309, creative play center, soccer field area and pavement area behind the building.

Valuables and Take Home Items

Everything students are taking home must be carried to Room 210 because students are not allowed back into their classroom.

Parent Pickup

Parents may pick up their children in Room 210. We will always plan on being in Room 210 from 5:15 p.m. to 5:30 p.m. If you arrive before 5:30 p.m., go to Room 210 and there will be a note on the door telling where we may be found.

Proper Dress

Students are asked to have their Zoe Fitness suit available every day. They will be given a chance to change after roll call is taken. Tennis shoes are required every day.

Snack

We will not be supplying snacks, but you may send one with your son/daughter if you wish. They will have a chance to eat at about 4:00 p.m.

Field trips

We will be taking field trips to places such as The Healing Center Bible Walk Through, Heller Park, Braums, etc. This will be done with parental notification and permission well in advance.

Planned Activities

There will be many fun activities, including relays (running, hopping, skipping, galloping, dribbling, scooters), tumbling (forward roll, backward roll, cartwheel, roundoff, etc.), seasonal sports skills, fitness development, table games, chess club (1 1/2 hours per week). There will be free play time on the playground, library time in morning only, classroom games and table tennis.

Expected Behavior

Every leader and helper is to be treated with respect. Students are to obey quickly and quietly. Students are to respect each other and each other's property. Students are to keep Room 210 and all other areas that we use neat and clean. Students are to listen to and follow all instructions given to them. Repeated failure to cooperate could result in a student being asked to withdraw from the program. Parents will be contacted if a challenge is present, and we will work together to resolve the situation before withdrawal is considered.

Enrollment

Child's Name:________________________________ Birthdate: ____________
Grade: ____________ (Last, First)
Parent's Name: ____
(Last, First)
Address:____
City:_____________________________State:_________ Zip:_______________
Home Phone: __________________Business Phone:_____________________
Person to call in case of emergency:/Phone

____
Mother/Father is: __ VBI Student __ VBI Staff __ VCS Staff __ VCS Parent __ VCC Staff __ Volunteer
If VCC or VCS Staff or volunteer, in what department do you work?

____
1. The child/student listed above will attend the following type of program:
Victory Enrichment for _______ hours
Victory Activities for ________1 hour (7-8 a.m.)
_______ 2 1/2 hours (3-5:30 p.m.)
_______ 3 1/2 hours (7-8 a.m. and 3-5:30 p.m.)

2. Participation in this program will be_______ Daily, Monday-Friday Other (Specify days): ____________________

NOTE: Since there is a limit on the number of children that Victory Enrichment can serve on a given day, priority consideration will be given to parents whose children will be enrolled in a daily program.

FEES: Annual non-refundable registration fee of $10 per student paid at the time of registration.

______Option 1: 1-5 Hour Ticket at $2.00 per hour

______Option 2: 6-30 Hour Ticket at $1.50 per hour.

These tickets will be purchased in advance on a need basis and punched as services are utilized. The ticket may be retained by the teacher to prevent misplacement of the ticket.

______Option 3: A monthly ticket at $1.25 per hour.

These tickets will be purchased in advance and retained by the teacher. Tickets may be purchased for the type of program selected.

______Hours Per Day 5 1/2 3 1/2 2 1/2

______FEE: $140 $131 $83 $60 $24

This monthly ticket is validated for a specified month only (It may not be carried over to another month.) If services start in the middle of the month, the parent must purchase a hourly ticket to be used until the start of the new month. A penalty fee of $2.00 will be assessed for any fraction of a hour a child remains (is not picked up) beyond the time agreed upon. This penalty fee must be paid before a parent is permitted to purchase additional tickets. Since Victory is not a licensed day care, children who are left beyond the 6-hour limit will be withdrawn from the program.

When you enroll in one of these programs you agree that your child(ren) WILL BE PERMITTED TO PARTICIPATE IN EITHER PROGRAM ONLY IF THEY HAVE A CURRENT PAID-IN-ADVANCE TICKET. If unable to purchase a monthly ticket, you may opt for a hourly ticket. Credit will not be permitted.

____

Parent Signature: Date:

Appendix N

Support-A-Winner

must supply new computers, videotape equipment, up-to-date library reference volumes and state-of-the-art science and foreign language laboratory equipment.

There are two ways to raise money for all these challenges: Either ask a few people to give a lot of money, or ask a lot of people to give a modest amount.

With your help, and with the help of many other generous supporters, Victory Christian School will have more than $130,000 to devote to its students this year! Please ask if your employer has a matching fund program. Your employer may donate a matching amount toward the total collected by the respective families.

Each family is asking 10 willing sponsors to give $55 or more in the next five months. Each family that reaches this goal receives their choice of a "Family Holiday" for four at a luxury hotel in Tulsa, Oklahoma, or a tuition discount.

The ***Top Achiever Family*** -- the family that gathers the most education dollars -- will receive a five-day expense paid vacation for four to **DisneyWorld and the Epcot Center in Orlando, Florida!** This family will also receive ***one year's paid tuition*** for one student at VCS, or an equivalent amount to be placed in a college education fund!

The next four runners' up -- the ***High Achiever Families*** -- will receive their **choice** of one of the following:

1. A weekend for four in beautiful San Antonio, Texas.
2. A one-year family membership at the Thornton YMCA in Tulsa, Oklahoma.
3. A $500 travel credit at Spears Travel Service.
4. One year's tuition at Victory Christian School.

Every organization and society on earth seeks top talent for their management, leadership and decision-making positions. Would YOU be interested in mediocre talent if you had a choice? Well you **do**!

We Train Our Students To Win, To Achieve, To Excel!

By investing $11 a month or more in a deserving young student at Victory Christian School for just five months **you** will receive the satisfaction of knowing you have invested in a sure thing -- your gift will go directly toward the Christian education of the next generation.

And you will receive a **tax-deduction receipt** for the full amount of your gift.

How Much Will Be Raised By This Program? Where Will The Money Be Spent?

The school expects to raise close to $130,000 through our dedicated families and their supportive sponsors.

The expenses of education fall into three broad categories. Tuition only covers a fraction of the cost incurred by:

1. Teaching Staff & Administrative Costs
2. Curriculum
3. Materials and Support Equipment

Teaching Staff & Administration

Every teacher at Victory Christian School is fully certificated with the State of Oklahoma. But we're not satisfied. We want to send our teachers to seminars and professional teachers' conventions to broaden and deepen our teachers' skill levels. We want to strengthen our benefits packages to keep the excellent teachers we have and to recruit even more as we grow.

Curriculum

Victory Christian School is constantly evaluating various curricula and techniques.

We are determined to **exceed** the student performance levels currently seen in most public and private schools. This requires current, up-to-date books, films, videotapes, and other expensive curriculum tools.

Materials & Support Equipment

We believe our children should have access to everything they need to emerge from this school fully equipped to compete and excel in college, on the job and in their personal and spiritual lives. To do this, we

(Over please)

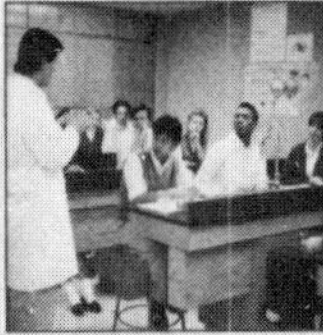

❑YES, I have enclosed a gift to ***Support A Winner*** at Victory Christian School:

- ❑ I have enclosed $55 with this coupon.
- ❑ I have enclosed $550 with this coupon.
- ❑ Other ____________

❑YES, I pledge to ***Support A Winner*** at Victory Christian School, but I want to send a total of:

- ❑ $550 or $110 per month over the next five months beginning ______ (Date).
- ❑ $110 or $22 per month over the next five months beginning ______ (Date).
- ❑ $55 or $11 per month over the next five months beginning ______ (Date).
- ❑ Other

Name ____________

Address ____________

City ____________

State ____________ Zip ____________

Family/Contact ____________

Relationship: ❑Relative ❑Friend ❑Business Associate ❑Other

Please mail this completed coupon with your gift to:
Victory Christian School
7700 S. Lewis
Tulsa, Oklahoma 74136

Please make all checks payable to Victory Christian School.

All gifts are tax deductible under IRS guidelines.

Index

V

W